The Beachcomber's Handbook
of Seafood Cookery

The Beachcomber's Handbook of Seafood Cookery

BY HUGH ZACHARY

Illustrated by Claude Howell

JOHN F. BLAIR, Publisher
Winston-Salem, N. C.

PRINTED IN THE UNITED STATES OF AMERICA
BY HERITAGE PRINTERS, INC.
CHARLOTTE, N. C.

This book is for my mother-in-law
LEE WIGGS
With Gratitude

ACKNOWLEDGMENTS

Many people made contributions to this book. I should like to thank, especially, Cap'n Larry Stubbs and all the other professional fishermen along the Southport waterfront who talked with me about the peculiarities of fish. Lewis Hardee knew much, much more than I did about shrimp; and "Cash" Caroon was a walking file of information about blue crabs. Information prepared by the North Carolina Agricultural Extension Service, the Public Information Office of the North Carolina Department of Conservation and Development, and the United States Department of the Interior also helped answer many questions.

Coastal restaurant owners, among them Louis Dixon and Mac McGlamery, not only prepare fine seafood but are free with their advice. And the ladies, bless 'em, had endless patience with an amateur seafood cook. I'm indebted to Mrs. Bessie Stubbs for advice and for several recipes and to Mrs. Thomas H. Watts, Mrs. A. K. McCallum, Mrs. Gilliam Hornstein, Mrs. E. C. Blake, and Mrs. Vivian Sparks. One of the best non-female seafood cooks I know, Pete Knight, passed along to me some of the better ideas in this collection.

Many other people talked with me during the preparation of this book, and their contributions were helpful. I'm sorry I can't mention all those who were asked, "What's your favorite seafood and how do you prepare it?" The cost of printing being what it is, we couldn't afford the extra one hundred pages; so my thanks will have to suffice.

CONTENTS

Author's Preface

I CAN SMELL AN OCEAN ACROSS A THOUSAND MILES OF DRY LAND, even though I didn't come eyeball to eyeball with one until I was almost an adult. A native midwesterner, I immediately fell in love with the low-lying marshlands, the numerous inlets and creeks, the wild life and marine life, the sandy beaches and the dunes, and everything about the Atlantic coastal area that is now my home.

It isn't that I want to be *on* the ocean. I have no ambition to cruise around the world in a canoe, and I think sails went out with clipper ships. Sailboats are cramped and damp, and they spring leaks at inconvenient times. Power boats are nice as long as they have a good mechanic aboard and a marine radio for yelling "Mayday! Mayday!" in case of fire or fog.

Of course, I always seem to be owned by some old hulk of a boat. I even have a Coast Guard license that allows me to carry not more than six passengers on a boat not exceeding fifteen tons in a restricted area along the Atlantic seaboard. This charter boat ticket entitles me to be addressed as Cap'n Zachary, but I don't insist on the formality among friends. In fact, I went in and out of the chartering business all in one summer. My current boat, the "Canto One," is just big enough to give me the confidence to run out along the Frying Pan Shoals or out to the sea buoy; and it will be rigged for loafing in the sun and for catching yellow-fin trout if I ever find time to finish the work.

Aside from the fact that salt air is good for my sinus condition, one of the main reasons why I like being near an ocean is seafood. Along the mid-Atlantic Coast, you'd be hard put to find Swedish shrimp or lobster thermidor or oysters Rockefeller; but the shrimp, oysters, and fish will be delicious, simple, and relatively unadorned. The residents of the seashore are people who know and appreciate the delicate shades of taste in fresh seafood, who don't believe in mucking up a fresh king mackerel fillet with sweet and sour fish sauce, who believe in preserving the natural flavor.

The success of such unembellished cookery is demonstrated, I feel, by the existence of the little settlement of Calabash, off Highway 17 just north of the South Carolina line. At this writing, a new seafood restaurant has just opened in Calabash, making a total of twelve restaurants in a town of less than one hundred people. The drawing power of the Calabash restaurants is their basic seafood platter, which is nothing more than a variety of common seafoods, mealed and fried lightly in deep fat. And Calabash is not an isolated phenomenon. Almost every North Carolina community within hailing distance of salt water has its seafood restaurant, and the menu of one is much like that of another.

People are willing to drive for miles to enjoy properly cooked fish, shrimp, and oysters. We used to make a Saturday evening by driving over a hundred miles from Fayetteville to the coast for dinner. To this date, one of my favorite Saturday night outings is a trip to Cap'n Jule's Hurricane Restaurant at Little River, where there's a guitarist-singer, a jug of wine, a pleasant atmosphere, a view of the mud flats and marsh and of the Intracoastal Waterway, and a seafood platter.

But this book is not intended to be a guide to seafood restaurants. It's designed for those who want to fry up a shore dinner at home or in the beach cottage, for those who might not know the best way to clean a particular fish, and for all who like things salty.

I have the good fortune to live in a very, very salty area—that east-west stretch of coastline on Long Bay below the Cape of Fear. Until the development of vacation facilities along the strands and industrial settlements here and there, the natives of the Lower Cape Fear area lived mainly by the sea. Such people know that there are not many creatures swimming or crawling in the ocean that don't make good eating if properly prepared. In my county, Brunswick, tidewater types have been cooking and eating seafood since the days when Sir John Yeamans attempted the first serious settlement on Old Town Creek in

1666. From those very early days, Brunswick cooks have merited the reputation of being able to make the most out of the least in raw materials.

In compiling the information, and possibly some misinformation, in this book, I've drawn liberally on the skills and knowledge of some of the older residents of the Lower Cape Fear. Some of the recipes that I've collected were developed in lean days when a man worked from before sunup until after dark and came home from the sea hungry enough to eat a horse and chase the driver. Such men were not hairy-chested sports fishermen. Often, they would sell the choice part of their catch and take the less desirable items home for the family table. From such people I've learned how to boil blue crabs, cut blowfish steaks, cook shark meat, make sea turtle stew, and fry rounds of skate wing.

We are rapidly becoming a nation of shore-seekers, and much of this book was written especially for the occasional visitor to the beaches. In addition, the swift transport of fresh seafood to inland cities puts a saltwater dinner close to most tables. Those who live inland and gather their clams and their oysters in the frozen-food center of a supermarket will miss, however, the sun and the salt and the glorious feeling of getting something for nothing that comes from discovering shellfish on a tidal flat; and, in all honesty, I don't know of a single item of seafare that improves with age. The over-all rule is: the fresher the better. But a two-day-old, carefully preserved fish is better than no fish at all.

But this book is more than just a cookbook. I have been fascinated by juicy tidbits of marine lore in my love affair with the Atlantic Coast of North Carolina and want to pass along some of the interesting things I have learned. For an old salt, much of the information contained in the material between recipes will be old stuff. However, to a refugee from Oklahoma and to others who have not spent their lives around salt water, many of the things taken for granted by natives are often new and puzzling.

The reader who bothers with the commentary between recipes will notice, along with some strong personal opinion, a flavor of conservation in my thinking. I flatly abhor waste. I regret the loss when a sports fisherman carries home a hundred pounds of mackerel from a charter fishing trip and lets it spoil because he's too tired to clean it. I don't even like to see a pier fisherman kill a skate or leave a scrap fish to die on the boards. Small fish, if tossed back into the water without too much injury, become big fish or food for big fish. All creatures have their function. The evil-looking skate is a living vacuum cleaner, keeping the ocean floor clean. The shark is the ocean's scavenger, performing the service of an underwater vulture. My motto is: if you're not going to eat it, don't kill it.

While preparing this book, I enjoyed learning about new ways to prepare familiar seafoods; and, especially, I took great interest in the odd and rare items. From the basic seafood plate to exotic dishes such as boiled octopus and baked squid, the recipes are designed to help along the amateur seafood cook and to give some new ideas to the old pro.

How to Make a Good Day
From a Bad Day's Fishing

THE BEACH SEASON BEGINS IN MAY AND ENDS WITH STARTLING suddenness the day after Labor Day. Thus, more people are enjoying salt air and sea breezes during the summer months than at any other time, and it follows that more people are looking for the ingredients of a seafood dinner during a time when there just ain't no fish.

The golden time for fishing is autumn, when the ocean seems to be alive with fish. In the autumn, after school openings around the state tie beach-going parents down to the old drag, after club and business activities return to normal following the summer slowdown, after most of the cottages along the strand are boarded and winterized, the beautiful days come to the beaches.

I am forced to admit a secret hope that people don't discover how wonderful autumn is along the coast. I enjoy the feeling of having the beach to myself after Labor Day. I'm selfish enough to want to be able to pitch my sun tent on the strand and look both ways for a quarter of a mile without seeing other people. I want to be able to cast my surf-fishing rig without fear of entanglement or to build a roaring fire behind a sand dune and roast a fat September mullet without having crowds of people kicking sand into the food as they pass. I can go happily through most of the summer without spending too much time along the strand itself; but when the humidity and temperature drop, when the mullet start south in a black stream just out past the first line of breakers, when the bluefish and mackerel are jumping in high, flashing arcs of motion in a flat, fall sea, when the spots are running and the puppy drum are hungry, that's my beach-going time. Autumn brings speckled trout, and the yellow-fin trout begin to eat anything you drop down to them out in the mouth of the river, and . . . .

I like autumn.

But the subject is summer and the unfortunate fact that, during the peak population time, the beach and the nearby ocean can resemble a desert, the only signs of life being white ghost crabs on the strand and white gulls overhead. Fish can be so scarce during the summer that bad days seem, to the summer vacationer, to be the rule.

Of course, offshore fishing can be fine during the vacation months. If the mackerel and bluefish are not out there, a charter boat skipper can load up his party with bottom fish—black sea bass and chicken snapper or, with longer trips to the edge of the Gulf Stream, red snapper and grouper.

On the shore, however, pickings can be lean on a hot, pretty, hungry, August day. On such a day every cottage along the strand will be full; the piers will be enjoying a landslide business; small boats will be cruising the waters inshore and offshore; and with the expenditure of thousands of dollars worth of pier tickets, equipment, and bait, with the squandering of endless hours of patience and energy, the take will consist of a couple of skates and a few blowfish. The skates will be stabbed and beaten on the bloody boards of the pier; and, chances are, the blowfish will be left to die on the same boards. Later, skate and blowfish carcasses will be kicked off the pier to feed the blue crabs.

On such days seafood restaurants do standing-room business, and hamburger stands have waiting lines. The vast richness of the sea fails to provide for the thousands of visitors who hope for fresh fish.

On such seemingly bankrupt days, it is possible to coax from the sea a meal that cannot be matched by any seafood restaurant —a good, solid meal with a pleasantly salty character, a meal to turn a bad day's fishing into a good day at the shore.

In the beginning, you might as well assume that fishing is going to be bad in, say, mid-August. You're going to fish, anyhow; but before you visit the pier or the local hot spot for fishing, make preparations for the big seafood dinner that you'd like to enjoy after your hard day. The menu you are hungry for might be something like this:

Oyster stew or clam chowder
Fresh fish steak
Scallops
Fresh crabmeat

But the season is closed on oysters, the tide isn't right for clamming, the fish are not biting, and there are no scallops. Let's take another look at that menu:

Coquina chowder
Fresh blowfish or shark steak
Scallops, made from rounded cuts of skate wing
Fresh crabmeat

Now, a little scavenging is in order. First, set the kids to picking coquinas from the beach. The coquina is a tiny bivalve which burrows in the sand near the low-tide mark. Although a very large coquina might be three-quarters of an inch long, the average coquina is about half an inch long. Coquina shells are colorful and gay. They may be barred or striped or show markings like radiating sun rays.

On the surface of it, gathering enough of the tiny shells for chowder for a family seems to be an impossible task. Actually, since coquinas are gregarious and are congregated in crowded areas just below the surface of the sand, it is possible to hand-pick enough in a very short time. An incoming tide, with waves washing lightly over a coquina bed, will show frenzied activity in the sand as the water runs off. The coquinas will be seen digging furiously to regain the security of the sand after a wave washes away their cover. In a large coquina colony, the sand will seem to be alive. Flashes of color will show as the living shells are exposed. Digging in the sand with the fingers will reveal dozens, hundreds, thousands of the colorful little bivalves.

Children usually love gathering coquinas—hence the suggestion to put them to work. If you want to make the task easier for them, a sifter made from a wooden frame and wire with a mesh of about ⅜ of an inch will enable one person to gather thousands of coquinas quickly.

The sifter is simply dipped into the sand. It's like panning gold, except that the reward is living shells rather than metal. Dip sand and shells into the sifter, rinse in the surf to wash the sand through the wire mesh, and pick out the larger pieces of dead shell before dumping the coquinas into a container.

Since the coquina is not the main bulk of the chowder but only a flavoring agent, it is not necessary to have massive amounts of the shells. A two-inch layer of living coquina shells in the bottom of the vessel used to cook the chowder should be enough. The flavor of the coquina is a rather powerful one; so, if there is a shortage of coquinas, as little as a half-inch layer of shells will add flavor to the mixture.

To prepare the coquina stock for chowder, wash the freshly gathered coquinas and pick out the larger pieces of dead shell and other trash. Smaller pieces of dead shell may be left with the coquinas. Place the washed shells in a pan, cover with water, and boil lightly until all living shells are open and tiny pieces of coquina meat have boiled loose from the shells and are floating in the water. Pour the liquid off into a container, leaving the empty shells in the bottom of the pan. The broth, with its tiny chunks of coquina meat, is to be used in the chowder. The broth may be prepared in advance and stored in the refrigerator. Real addicts of coquina chowder have been known to prepare and freeze quarts of broth for use at a later date.

With the coquina broth ready, more scavenging is needed to round out the menu. The fishermen in the family may, by this time, be convinced that the fish are not going to bite; or they may have landed a half-dozen ugly, unappetizing blowfish. Sometimes, when the fish are not biting, even blowfish will not bite well; and it will be necessary, in order to provide fresh fish steaks for the table, to walk up and down the pier and collect fresh blowfish from other fishermen who are leaving them to die on the boards of the pier. (This, too, might be a good job for the children.) Most fishermen are only too willing to have someone carry away the ugly blowfish. And they will think you're crazy when you ask for a freshly caught skate before they stab it to ribbons and throw it back for the crabs. However, to round out the menu, you'll need about two blowfish per person and one good-sized skate.

The blowfish, like most fish, carries a variety of local names. He's called blowtoad, puffer, toadfish, swellfish, and you-so-and-so-get-off-my-hook. As with any fish other than one of the more famous species such as the king mackerel, it's difficult to reconcile the local names with the names one finds in authoritative fish identification books. As near as I can make out, our blowfish is the checkered puffer. At any rate, the blowfish, if tickled, will puff himself up so that his tummy is rounded like a ball. His skin is rough to the touch. If in doubt, ask the nearest grizzled old-timer if this puffer is the fish that has the two delicious little chunks of white meat on either side of his spine.

The puffer is caught on bottom rigs from piers or boats or in the surf. His skin, viscera, and roe are poisonous. In some Pacific species, the poison is quite potent. There are fatalities in Japan each year from puffer poisoning. Japanese cooks who prepare puffer meat for consumption by the public are required to graduate from a special cooking school. However, the puffer caught along the mid-Atlantic Coast is quite safe if care is taken in cleaning it. There are people who say they would rather have blowfish steak than any other fish swimming, and they insist that they would have been dead long since if the blowfish were dangerously poison.

However, I will repeat the warning that is included in every reference book I've checked: *The skin, roe, and viscera of the blowfish are poisonous.*

In proper cleaning, it is not necessary to puncture the stomach of the blowfish. Tools needed are a sharp knife and, if one becomes a blowfish enthusiast, a pair of sharp-pointed scissors.

With the fish lying on its stomach, cut off the tail at the point of junction with the body. Cut off the fin on top of the fish. With the knife or scissors, make a lengthwise slit in the tough skin from tail to head. Peel the skin down the sides of the fish, exposing the solid, white chunk of meat along the backbone. Cut off the head with a sharp knife. Head, skin, and stomach will then fall away, leaving the steak and backbone. At this point, it is optional whether or not to cut the steak away from the backbone. One school of thought states that the meat is sweeter and juicier when cooked bone in. The other prizes the rather delicate flavor of blowfish steak. Its followers fillet the meat away from the backbone to leave only the boneless, white chunks.

Incidentally, blowfish freezes well. Milk cartons make excellent freezing containers. The fresh flavor of the fish is best maintained when the meat is covered with water before freezing.

The alternate fish dish is shark steak. Any small shark will do. Sharks caught in inland waters or from a fishing pier may be of the dogfish or sand shark variety. Local names differ. One small shark often caught in the Cape Fear River is called the "river shark." Trying to match local names with the scientific names is a task for a scholar, not a fisherman who hasn't had a great catch. In general, any shark caught along the Atlantic Coast is good to eat. Of course, the smaller the shark, the more tender the meat.

Cleaning a shark is simple, if one is careful of the skin, which is sandpaper tough. First, draw the shark and cut off the hard bristle tail portion. Skin the shark before or after cutting him crosswise into steaks. Cut steaks about one-half inch thick for frying and about one inch thick for baking.

Shark meat is cooked just like any other fish. It may be fried, baked, or used in any way that other fish are used.

Now, let's tackle another rough-looking product of the sea that makes fine eating—the skate. There are many varieties of skates and rays. Along the mid-Atlantic Coast, the chances of catching some exotic type of ray are slim. The lesser electric ray is said to be present in waters from North Carolina south; but I have never seen one, nor have I found any of the older fishermen who have. The electric ray is spotted and has two sail-like fins on a broad, flat tail.

Chances are about fifty-fifty that the fisherman will catch a common stingray instead of a skate. While shapes may vary, the stingray family usually have long, slender tails with one or more spike-like barbs on them. The stingray is the subject of much dispute. I've read supposedly authoritative sources which state flatly that there is a venom on the barb of a stingray. I've read equally authoritative texts which state flatly that the barb of a stingray does not have venom and that it is said to be poisonous only because it is capable of inflicting a deep puncture wound that becomes infected easily because of the slime and filth on the stingray's barb. The last authoritative text I read explains that the venom sacs are nonrenewable and are contained in grooves along the spike, under an outer skin. When the spike is rubbed hard against something, such as a shrimp net, or jammed into something, such as a swimmer's foot, the outer skin and poison sacs are dislodged. Thus, it is possible for one person to be stabbed by a stingray and suffer only a puncture wound, while another receives a dose of venom.

I think it's wise to assume that stingrays do have venom unless the poison sacs are missing from the barb.

I've not been able to find anyone who has eaten stingrays. "Don't get tangled up with a stingray," I've been told.

But, apparently, anything one catches in the way of a skate or a ray that does not have a stinger is edible. Actually, there will be little question in your mind about which varieties are edible, once the specimen is in the boat or on the pier. A skate generally has a thick tail. The tail will be barbless; and by this I mean that there will be no nail-like spike sticking out of it. If the catch is huge, say more than two feet from wingtip to wingtip, it's probably not a skate but some variety of ray. My experience with skates is limited, although I can testify to the fact that properly prepared skate is as fine as anything I've eaten from the sea.

Those with more experience tell me that the smaller the skate, the more tender the meat. This makes sense. A skate, with no barb on its tail and under two feet in wingspan, is what we're after.

A freshly caught skate is a lively thing and, sometimes, seemingly indestructible. He may be killed by stabbing him between the eyes with a stout knife or by clubbing him briskly with a belaying pin or its equivalent.

The edible portion of the skate is in the wings. With a sharp knife, sever the wings from the body. With the wings held firmly on a cleaning board, score the skin into strips of one to two inches. With fingers or pliers, strip the tough outer skin away. Repeat the process on the other side, leaving the white flesh of the wings. Cut the strips of meat into squares. If you want to fool a guest and make him think he's eating scallops, round the corners of the squares.

Moving toward a seafood dinner that makes the most of a bad day's fishing, we have coquina broth prepared, ready to make chowder; and we have blowfish or shark and skate wing ready for cooking. Fresh crabmeat is one of the easiest to obtain of all seafoods and one of the most diverting, especially for the youngsters. Crabs can be taken almost anywhere there is salt water. We cover them completely in another chapter.

Now let's cook our seafood dinner.

Coquina Chowder

1

Coquina broth (about six cups)   *2 teaspoons flour*
3 small slices salt pork   *1 or 2 onions, diced*
1 cup milk

Fry pork until brown and remove pork from pan. Mix flour in fat. Add broth and onions. Cook about thirty minutes, or until onions are done. Add milk and reheat.

2

Coquina broth (about one quart)	*1 onion, diced*
	Salt and pepper
2 medium-sized potatoes, cubed	*1 carrot, diced*
	3 or 4 slices salt pork

Fry pork until crisp and brown and remove pork from pan. Add broth, potatoes, onions, carrots, and seasonings and cook until potatoes are soft. Water may be added.

NOTE: Coquina chowder is one of those do-it-by-feel dishes. The amount of coquinas may vary. The amount of potatoes may vary. And you may leave off everything and just drink the broth. Leaving the fatback, or salt pork, out of the recipes will limit the taste to that of the flavoring coquinas. Body may be added to the chowder by increasing the amount of flour or by mixing a paste of cornmeal and water and adding it to the chowder. Onions may be left out or increased.

Blowfish Steak

Blowfish steaks (bone in or filleted)	*½ cup flour, meal, or both*
	½ teaspoon salt
Black pepper to taste	

In skillet or deep fryer, heat cooking oil to about 375°. Roll steaks in mealing mixture to which salt and pepper have been added and fry until done, about five minutes, turning once.

NOTE: When frying puffers or toadfish or blowfish—whatever you've decided to call them—remember that the flavor is delicate and is best appreciated when they are cooked in fresh oil. When cooked with other fish or in oil that has been used for cooking other fish, the blowfish tends to take on a stronger flavor.

Fried Shark Steaks

Shark steaks	*Mealing mixture*
Black pepper	*Salt*

Roll or shake steaks in mixture of flour or meal, black pepper, and salt. Fry in deep fat about five minutes.

Baked Shark Steaks

Shark steaks	*Melted butter or fat*
Salt	*Bacon (optional)*

Dry fish on paper towels. Rub with salt and place in greased baking pan. Brush with butter or fat. Lay bacon slices over top. Bake in moderate oven for forty to sixty minutes, or until meat flakes easily. Baste occasionally.

For those who dislike waste, who want to utilize leftovers or make use of all the meat brought home by the fisherman, fishcakes are excellent. In the following recipe, leftover shark steak or skate wing morsels can be used; or almost any kind of fish can be substituted, either cooked or raw.

Fishcakes with Skate or Shark

Shark steak or skate wing	*1 large egg*
* morsels (about two cups)*	*1 cup soft bread crumbs or*
1 tablespoon onion, grated	* mashed potatoes*
1 tablespoon lemon juice	*½ teaspoon salt*
Black pepper	

Grind fresh shark steak or skate wing morsels in meat grinder. Boil for fifteen minutes and drain. Combine all ingredients. Shape into croquettes or patties. Fry at 375°, with cooking oil covering about one-half of patties, until brown. Turn and brown other side.

NOTE: It may be necessary, in order to keep patties from crumbling, to add two tablespoons of flour to the mixture. If leftover meat is used, light browning is all that is necessary, since the meat is already cooked.

Scalloped Skate

Skate wing morsels, square or   Mealing mixture of salt,
    rounded   pepper, and meal or flour
            1 egg, beaten in canned milk

Dip skate wing morsels into milk-egg mixture and roll in mealing mixture. Deep fry about five minutes at 375°.

IF IT'S A REALLY BAD DAY

There are those who don't like to fish and who can't, perhaps, stomach the thought of skate wings or shark steak or coquina chowder. There are those who are visiting the beach mainly for the sun and the surf and who don't want to use valuable time preparing food and cooking, and there are those who are spending only one afternoon or evening at the beach. For ease of preparation, it's hard to beat what I call the lazy man's beach dinner of clams, yams, and corn. This dinner is ideal for a day of surf or inlet fishing, for a day of lazing in the sun on the strand, or for a moonlight beach party. Aside from fresh clams, sweet potatoes, and fresh corn on the cob, the only requirements are a fire, a metal can of the type sold very cheaply by fish houses and other waterfront establishments, and an appetite.

The cooking vessel, a five-gallon "lard" can, can be used over and over, of course; or the fishermen can use it after the meal to carry home the catch. Clams can almost always be found in a tidal flat or, in emergencies, bought from a seafood market; and there are usually fresh vegetable stands along the approaches to the beaches where the other ingredients can be purchased. The dinner can be served in the open air without eating utensils, or indoors.

Steamed Clams, Yams, and Roastin' Ears

Fresh clams   *Roasting ears of corn, shucked*
Small sweet potatoes, washed

Layer ears of corn in bottom of lard can (or any cooker if meal is prepared indoors). Layer sweet potatoes over corn, and clams in shell over potatoes. Pour in about one quart water. Close lard can and punch small hole in top. Cook until steam stops coming out of the hole.

Cooking may be done over an open fire or over any other source of heat. For large parties, layers may be repeated, adding approximately one quart of water for each composite layer of yams, clams, and corn. As the clams are opened by the steam, their juices run down and permeate the corn and yams, making for a taste that, when enjoyed under a warm, friendly sun or a full, glowing moon on a lonely strand, is purely out of this world. Usually, you'll find that no salt or other seasoning is needed. However, having a bit of salt and pepper and some butter on hand is a matter of personal option. The beauty of the dinner is its simplicity for outdoor use; but the first time I ate it, it was used as the main course of a formal, very delicious dinner in a stately old home in Wilmington, so it is very much at home indoors as well.

Of All the Fish
That Swim or Swish

I DON'T KNOW ALL ABOUT FISH. IN FACT, I'M PROBABLY ONE OF THE
world's worst fishermen. I've tried, for example, to catch a
speckled trout for five years now. Experienced trout fishermen
go to Lockwood Folly Inlet in the fall and catch speckled trout.

Others take speckled trout in the creeks around Bald Head Island. I once saw a speckled trout caught and, on that same eventful day, I hooked what might have been a speckled trout; but he got off before I could boat him. If I approach Lockwood Folly Inlet, the trout stop biting. They may have been chewing up the lures and live bait for half an hour, but they cease all activity when I start walking toward the water with a rod in my hand and malice in my heart.

It's that way with speckled trout. Cap'n Larry, one of the best trout fishermen of the Lower Cape Fear area, has given up on me. He refuses to take me speckled trout fishing with him any more. He was with me the day I hooked into what might have been a speckled trout; and he was the one who caught the one speckled trout ever caught in my presence; and the trout, seeing its grave mistake, bit him.

I once stopped a massive white-bass run below one of the huge TVA dams near Knoxville, Tennessee. When I parked at the top of the bank leading down toward the water, dozens of happy fishermen were hauling in white bass by the hundreds. By the time I got my tackle out of the car and climbed down the rocks, the run had stopped. The last fish came ashore when I was five feet from the water, and that was it.

Now it's a different story with gray trout. With gray trout, I'm a killer. All of the affection that I don't lavish on speckled trout I reserve for gray trout. I'm also quite fond of croakers, for they seem to like me. I may not be the champion croaker fisherman in this area, but I'd be right up there near the top if you measure the qualities of us croaker fishermen by results alone. I've never gone after croakers when I didn't get all I wanted. I suppose that's because the croaker is always with us, will bite just about anything, and will, if the fisherman isn't sharp enough, hook himself. I've also had moderate success with bluefish when they are inshore on the shoals, and I can load a boat with black-fish any time from spring to late winter.

The only thing that saves me from being a complete bust at surf fishing is a historic catch of a thirty-five-pound red bass; but this was in Florida and shouldn't be listed as an accomplish-ment, I suppose, since this book deals with fish of the Carolina coast. I did catch a whiting in the surf once. I was lying on a blanket under a tent to keep out of the sun, with a cold beer in my hand, music on the radio, and a surf rod in a holder with the bait washed almost ashore by the action of the waves, when a crazy whiting who didn't know he wasn't supposed to come all the way up on shore hooked himself and stayed on with grim determination until I pulled him in. I was so grateful to the fish that I released him; but since he obviously had a death wish, I'm sure he was the one caught by a serious fisherman five minutes later a few yards down the strand.

The point of all this is: I'm not a complete angler. I just eat fish. A lot of my information about fish has been collected from people who catch fish for a living and from people who have lived near the coast and lived off the water for years. Not only am I not a serious fisherman; I am a relative newcomer to salt water. In my defense, I will say that I learn fast; and I love the water enough to have studied it a bit. I hold a Coast Guard license that qualifies me to operate a boat under fifteen gross tons while carrying six or less passengers. At one time I had my boat up for hire and carried a few charters until I decided that the responsibility of caring for, and of finding fish for, six strangers was not for me. A charter boat skipper has to be made of stern stuff. There are days when there just ain't no fish, and those are the bad days. When a group of men drive a hundred

or so miles to catch a fish, pay out a lot of good dollars, get up
at three o'clock in the morning, and go all day without catching one single bluefish or mackerel or anything, it gets rather
chilly on deck before the boat can be guided home to the dock.
Of course, this happens occasionally to the best of skippers, for
fish are notoriously independent. I just don't have the stomach
for it. If I made my living from the sea, it wouldn't be by charter
fishing. It would be by trapping blackfish or by some similar
activity so that when the fish were not there, it wouldn't dis-
appoint anyone but me.

The life of a charter skipper is a good life but a rough one,
and it doesn't make a man rich. The days are long. I'm more
familiar, at least in recent years, with the Southport charter
fleet than with any other. One of the main problems here is
lack of publicity. As far as the upstate papers are concerned,
there seems to be only one saltwater area in North Carolina,
beginning with the Outer Banks and ending at the Morehead-
Beaufort area. I've fished out of Morehead City, Sneads Ferry,
the Wilmington beaches, Little River, and Southport; and although the fishing is good everywhere, I think the Southport
boats catch fish as consistently as any of them. As a matter of
fact, some of the boats from farther north run down the coast
and end up fishing in the waters off the Cape Fear. I realize
that one of the main reasons for the lack of publicity for Lower
Cape Fear boats is the simple lack of a publicity pipeline. The
promoters around the Banks have done a tremendous job over
the years, bringing that area from relative obscurity to national
prominence. However, it would be nice if the news media upstate would realize, now and then, that the Frying Pan Shoals,
extending from Bald Head out toward the Frying Pan Light
Tower, are among the state's finest fishing grounds. Several

times I've seen newspaper headlines saying, "First Sailfish of the Season" or "First Marlin Caught"; yet there had been a billfish on the Southport docks a week or two before.

Now that I've ground that ax, still trying to make up in some way for my weaknesses in fishing lore, a word about seasons. Fall is fishing time. In the fall there are trout and spots and mullet and whiting and blues and mackerel and drum. Spring has its points, with blues and mackerel and dolphin offshore; and those who are determined, or who hire an experienced charter skipper, can even catch fish in the summer; but fall is the time when almost anyone, even I, can catch fish.

The gray trout, or yellow-fin trout as he's called locally, is my favorite. Of course, yellow-fin fishing is bottom fishing; and some people who consider themselves real sportsmen turn up their noses at baiting a hook with a piece of dead shrimp and letting a sinker carry the bait to the bottom. I, too, enjoy the feel of a big kingfish or a fighting bluefish when a trolling lure is hit; but I suppose I'm more a meat fisherman than a sporting fisherman. I'd never mount a sailfish, for example. If I were not going to eat him, I'd turn him loose. Ditto for everything down to and including the most insignificant pinfish. When I fish for yellow-fin trout, I'm enjoying the fall sun and the cool breeze; and I'm also looking forward to a fresh trout fillet for dinner.

There are charter parties who say they are not interested in bottom fishing. There are no game fish around, so the skipper, who believes that the paying customer is boss, pulls lures around the ocean all day and catches, maybe, two small bluefish. The price of those fish is about fifty dollars a pound. And the skipper could have put his party onto some good fish rocks where they could, by bottom fishing, have caught some very edible items such as blackfish or chicken snapper.

I realize, of course, that fishing is sort of a religion. And I know it's more fun to fight in a big king than to reel up a one-pound black bass from the bottom. I just believe in being practical.

I'm going to try to make a list of the edible marine species that one is likely to encounter in North Carolina and vicinity. This list may not be complete. If there are any gross inaccuracies, blame the writer and not those with whom he has talked, nor the authors of the books on which he has leaned heavily: Harden F. Taylor, *Survey of Marine Fisheries of North Carolina* (Chapel Hill: The University of North Carolina Press, 1951), and Hugh M. Smith, *The Fishes of North Carolina*, Volume II of *North Carolina Geological and Economic Survey* (Raleigh: E. M. Uzzell and Company, State Printers and Binders, 1907).

EDIBLE SALTWATER FISH

Flounder: In North Carolina, mostly the summer or Southern flounder. Caught from piers or in creeks and inlets; gigged in shallow water; or taken in nets in deep, offshore water in cold weather. Probably the most prized of all fish for eating because of its firm, sweet flesh and lack of bones. Small flounder up to about eight inches in size are usually cooked bone in after scaling, drawing, and cutting off the head. Larger flounder are usually filleted.

Speckled Trout: Also called sea trout, salmon trout, spotted weakfish, spotted squeteague, Southern squeteague, and, by the author, * * * * * *! Mostly a fall fish. Caught on live bait or on artificial lures in inlets, at the mouths of creeks, and in gill nets on the strand. Very good eating fish. Flesh is soft; thus the name weakfish. Usually filleted for cooking.

Gray Trout: Also called yellow-fin trout, sea trout, summer trout, weakfish, squeteague, shad trout, sun trout, and Sweet Thang—mostly by Cap'n Larry, the best yellow-fin trout fisherman of the Lower Cape Fear. Taken on shrimp on the bottom of rivers and creeks and offshore. Primarily a fall fish, but begins to show up three to five miles offshore on good coral rock bottom as early as mid-July. One of the finest eating fish. Flesh, like that of the speckled trout, is soft. Fish at about one pound each are usually filleted. Smaller specimens may be fried bone in.

Spot: So called because of a round black spot on its shoulder.

A rather small fish, averaging less than half a pound. Taken during bottom fishing in the summer, but primarily a fall fish, running in huge schools. When spot fishing is good, it's very good on piers, in the surf, and in inlets and rivers. Spots are deep fried in the round by confirmed spot eaters. Other people dress spots by scaling, drawing, and cutting off head and tail. Smoked spot is among the Western world's finer seafood treats.

Croaker: Also called hardhead. Name comes from the croaking sound fish makes when boated. The croaker is the fish for fishermen who never catch fish. He's around in rivers, creeks, and inlets from early spring through fall. He bites almost anything, especially shrimp, during bottom fishing. A half-pound croaker would be a tremendous specimen. Although small, the croaker is not to be sneezed at as a food fish. Millions of pounds of croaker are marketed each year. Dress by scaling, cutting off head and tail, and drawing out stomach and contents.

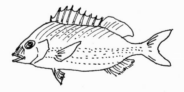

Pigfish: Caught wherever croakers are caught. Vertically thick fish with low-slung, small-mouthed head. Makes noise somewhat like croaker when boated. Good eating. To clean, scale, draw, and cut off head and tail.

Whiting: Also called sea mullet. A small-mouthed fish, looking much like a mullet, which is taken during bottom fishing in the surf and in rivers, sounds, and inlets. May be filleted, if about a pound in size; or dress by scaling, drawing, and cutting off head and tail.

Mullets: Summer mullets taken in nets in creeks or sounds are jumping mullet or silverside mullet. Usually rather small. Dress by scaling, drawing, and cutting off head and tail. The September mullet, some heavy with roe, run much larger and can be filleted or pan-dressed. Fresh mullet is a good tasting fish.

Drums: The red drum is one of the most respected game fishes of the surf and inlets. Called redfish, red bass, or spotted-tail bass (for the spot just forward of the tail), the red drum grows to an impressive size. Small red drum, below about five pounds, are known as puppy-drum. Large specimens are steaked or fillet steaked. Smaller ones may be pan cleaned by scaling, drawing, and cutting off head and tail. Red drum and puppy-drum are excellent food fish.

The black drum, a small fish of a different species that looks somewhat like a sheephead, is taken in creeks and inlets in the fall and early winter. Some true saltwater types say that the black drum "ain't fit to eat." Black-drum eaters say they don't bother with the larger ones but use only the smaller fish.

Pompano: Caught infrequently in rivers, in the surf, and in inland waters. Highly prized, pompano is usually the highest-priced fish on the fresh-fish market. Sometimes taken offshore during bottom fishing.

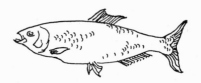

Shad: A specialty fish, taken usually in nets during the spring spawning run. Before the mid-thirties, the shad was North Carolina's most important commercial fish. There are those who say that the shad is the best of all fish for eating.

Herring: A small, bony fish which comes into rivers and creeks in the spring. Some say it's the world's worst fish. Usually deep fried whole, it is eaten bones and all.

Sheephead: Also called sheepshead. Caught around old pilings and, offshore, around wrecks. Sheephead fishing is something of a specialty. Adepts say you have to "jerk just before the sheephead bites" to catch him. His favorite bait is the fiddler crab.

Sturgeon: Now and then a sturgeon is taken in a net in a river or sound. Usually he is released because of his size and his unappetizing looks. Old-timers, however, say that the sturgeon makes very good eating. Hard to clean because of its tough hide, it is skinned in strips, after cutting into the indentations between the ridges on its side.

DEEP WATER FISH

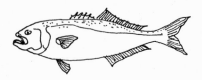

Bluefish: Most plentiful in the fall, but caught in great numbers during the spring migration and throughout the summer. Mostly a blue-water fish and a prime target of North Carolina charter boats, the blue is also taken from piers, in inlets, and in rivers. A voracious feeder, the blue hits artificial lures, live bait, and at times even cut bait or shrimp during bottom fishing. Small blues, traveling in huge, hungry schools and taking bait as fast as it can be fed to them, are called skipjacks. The blue cleans easily. His stomach is small and can be drawn easily, and he has scales that are very easily removed. Larger blues, above a pound, may be filleted.

King Mackerel: Also called kingfish or cero. Larger cousin of the Spanish mackerel. When a charter boat hits a school of kings, it's jackpot day. Spring and fall, with occasional catches through the summer, usually offshore. Some kings are caught from fishing piers in spring and fall by float fishing. A day spent reeling in large kings is a hard day's work. Usually steaked or fillet steaked. Fine for smoking, baking, frying, or broiling.

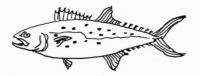

Spanish Mackerel: The Spanish mackerel is another mainstay of charter boats. Skippers start looking for mackerel and blue-fish in early spring, sometimes as early as mid-April. The Spanish travel in schools, and—as in the case of bluefish—it's usually feast or famine. Usually filleted or steaked. Easy to clean.

Atlantic Mackerel: Also called mackerel, blue mackerel, or Boston mackerel. A more northern species which is sometimes caught in the spring off North Carolina. Steaked or fillet steaked, the Atlantic mackerel is one of the world's finest food fish.

Dolphin: This beautiful, rainbow-hued fish with the high fore-head and the long dorsal fin is a real fighter on a hook. Taken offshore in blue water, the dolphin is an excellent food fish. Steaked or fillet steaked.

Sailfish: The sail makes him one of the glamour fishes for big-time anglers. Millions of tons of good fish have been wasted in mounting sailfish. Usually steaked, the sailfish is as good as any fish swimming.

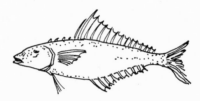

Cabio: Also called cobia or coal fish. A large, offshore fish resembling a catfish. Also runs into bays, inlets, and channels. Steaked or fillet steaked.

Marlin: Blue marlin and white marlin are taken by trolling off the mid-Atlantic Coast. These huge fish are good eating when steaked.

Swordfish: Swordfish steak is a gourmet food.

Wahoo: Caught offshore or in Gulf Stream. Good eating. Steaked or fillet steaked.

Barracuda: This people-eater is also delicious when eaten by people. Large barracuda may be steaked or fillet steaked.

Permit: Rarely seen. When caught, usually precipitates arguments about what it is. Has yellow fins, a blunt nose, a low-slung mouth, and a whitish belly. Very good eating.

Albacore: Member of the tuna family. Edible. Steaked.

OFFSHORE BOTTOM FISH

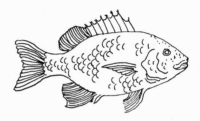

Red Snapper: Highly regarded. May be filleted or fillet steaked. Medium-sized specimens may be baked whole after drawing and scaling.

Blackfish: Also called black bass or black sea bass. A staple for northern seafood markets. Thousands of pounds are taken in traps for commercial sale, beginning about September and continuing throughout the winter when most fish are scarce. Takes the hook with voracious eagerness from early spring through very late winter, or as long as anyone wants to drop a hook to it. Moves offshore into deeper water when cold weather settles in. Small blackfish are caught during bottom fishing in rivers, creeks, and sounds. Larger fish may be filleted. Small blackfish are pan-dressed by drawing, scaling, and cutting off head and tail.

Chicken Snapper: The porgy. Delicious fish of the rocky bottoms offshore. Usually filleted. (Not to be confused with the spadefish, often also called porgy and also good eating.)

Hog Snapper: Looks much like the smaller pigfish of the inland waters. Long snout and small mouth. Usually filleted.

Grouper: This sometimes monstrous fish is usually steaked or chunked.

SOME FISH NOT USUALLY EATEN

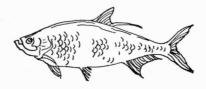

Tarpon: One of the most prized game fish, but said to be completely unappetizing.

Amberjack: "Wormfish." Waterfront authorities say that the amberjack has a set of nerves or muscles which look so much like worms that they might as well be worms. The author is in the dark as to whether the amberjack is not eaten because he doesn't taste good or because of the "worms."

Jack Cavally: Also called jack cavalla or crevallé. When deep-sea fishermen types are asked why no one eats the jack cavally, they shrug and say nothing. He just isn't eaten. I suppose someone has tried at one time or another, however.

Bonito: Also called false albacore. Has a dark, reddish meat. Usually used for cut bait.

THE MOST FISHED FOR FISH IN THE SEA

Two billion pounds a year: that's a catch. Menhaden, called pogies or fatback, run in schools, eat tiny plant organisms, and can be made into a nutritious, high-protein meal that is currently being promoted as an answer to hunger in the underdeveloped parts of the world. And two billion pounds of pogies make quite a stink when they're processed into fish meal or oil at plants scattered up and down the coast.

Menhaden aren't often eaten, although some crewmen of the menhaden ships salt down menhaden for winter consumption. In the late 1890's, menhaden were selling on the Boston fresh-food markets for ten cents apiece for table consumption.

I don't have a recipe for preparing menhaden, in view of my lack of contact with those menhaden eaters in Boston in the late nineteenth century, but some skimpy information is available. Menhaden were cooked without cooking oil of any kind in the pan, for the menhaden is a rather oily fish. As for salting, I suppose menhaden are salted much as other fish are salted.

I should think that "planking" a menhaden might be feasible, if one were hungry enough. A large specimen—and they grow up to about eighteen inches—with the oil baked out on a plank might be fit to eat.

Of one thing I am sure: pogy roe is very fine eating. Louis Dixon serves pogy roe in season at his seafood restaurant in Southport, deep-frying it after mealing. It has a more solid, more appetizing taste than most fish roe.

In the early Massachusetts colony, settlers used menhaden oil as a substitute for the more expensive whale oil. Menhaden oil is highly unsaturated in fat content. Perhaps it will be used someday as a substitute for fats that build the cholesterol level in the blood.

Netting menhaden, from ships that are generally converted minesweepers, is an interesting operation. Smaller boats pull the huge purse net into a circle, trapping the schooling menhaden inside. Few game fish are caught, for they are swift enough to escape the slow-moving net. Blues and mackerel will feed around the edge of a dense school of menhaden, but old menhaden fishermen say that a closely-packed school of menhaden exudes an acid or some other substance that kills any game fish venturing inside the fringes of the school. If this is true, and I suspect it has some foundation, for I've never seen game fish in a school of menhaden—only around the edges—I would want to have the inside position in a school if I were a menhaden. I've seen bluefish go into a feeding frenzy—like Jacques Cousteau's sharks on television—continuing to slash and cut menhaden even after their small stomachs were full.

Why so much about menhaden when they are rarely eaten? I suppose because there are two menhaden reduction plants across the marsh from my house; and when the wind is due north on a work day, the smell is ripe, thus making me more aware of menhaden. Or, perhaps, I'm preparing for the future, when we've used up our more pleasant marine resources and when high-protein fish meal has become a staple in all of our diets. Drive by a menhaden plant in operation, breathe deeply of the smell, and consider the wisdom of conservation. I suppose that is a message of some sort. One of the esthetic objections to high-protein fish meal, as now constituted, is the little matter of grinding *all* of the fish—hide, hair, guts, and everything—into the delicious mixture. Good, though. At least, according to those Washington folks who are trying to sell the idea of fish meal to the starving peoples of the world.

LET'S CLEAN A FISH

Take a croaker. Almost anyone can take a croaker. You can clean him with a knife as your only weapon. However, I highly recommend a fish-scaler. A fish-scaler is nothing much more than a serrated edge. Mine is a dime-store contraption which is a combination potato-peeler and scaler. Some fish knives are made with a sharp blade on one side and a serrated edge for scaling on the other. I have two friends, both avid fishermen, who own electric scalers. One of them also owns a battery-powered, self-propelled fish lure. I don't think either is necessary for the average fisherman. A good hand-scaler will do the job.

Hold the croaker by the head. Scrape the scaler against the grain of the scales until the fish is smooth. Next, cut off the tail. Cut off the head, by making a slanting cut from behind the gills forward to the back of the head, thus saving the part-ounce of meat at the front of the backbone. To draw, insert point of knife in anal opening on bottomside of fish and cut forward. This motion usually carries the intestines with it. If not, run the thumbnail down the body cavity to remove all intestines and linings.

Wash fish thoroughly, being careful to remove the small amount of blood from the cleaned body cavity, using thumbnail to push out remaining cavity linings.

Fish are best cleaned outside. Around most waterfronts, you can find fish-cleaning tables where scraps can be dumped directly into the water or put into disposal bins. Fishing is hard, hot work. Getting ready to go fishing is tough enough—packing all the gear, stowing it in the boat, putting the boat in the water, etc. Coming back is sheer torture; for the gear must be cleansed of salt spray and water, and the boat must be rinsed down and secured or taken out of the water. And then there are the cotton-pickin' fish to be cleaned. I've been known to fish all day and turn back everything I caught just so I wouldn't have to clean it. That was, of course, when I had plenty of fish in the freezer.

Actually, cleaning fish isn't all that bad. Oh, it takes a while to get the fish smell off your hands, but soda will help. And the sooner you clean a fish after he's caught, the fresher he's going to taste. That's why I recommend the use of fish-cleaning tables on the scene. Also, cleaning the fish there eliminates messing up the kitchen at home.

It is intimidating as all heck to come back from a deep-sea trip with a hundred and fifty Spanish mackerel and have to face cleaning them. At such times, you'll see eager young people around crying out, "Clean your fish, mister?" It's a fine answer to a problem, for it's hard work fighting a hot rod and reel all day. Let the youngsters clean your fish. If you don't, the poor little tykes probably won't have enough money to put gas in their new Mustangs.

For the complete greenhorn—if, for example, your fishing or nonfishing wife starts making the mighty meat-hunter of the family clean his own cotton-pickin' fish—there are a couple of terms that may need explaining.

In the Round: A fish just as Mother Nature made him.

Drawn Fish: Only the entrails have been removed. If the fishing day is to be a long one, or if the fish have to be transported home before cleaning, drawing fish while on the water will preserve their fresh flavor.

Dressed or Pan-dressed: Fish that have been scaled, drawn, and headed. Tail and fins may or may not be removed. With small fish, it's sometimes best to leave fins to help hold the small bones in place.

Fillets: All meat. The side of the fish cut away from the bone. To fillet, first scale fish. With a sharp knife, slice side of fish away from backbone. Cut from tail or from head, whichever works out better for you.

Fillet Steaks: Fillets of large fish cut into smaller pieces.

Steaks: Cross sections of fish of good size. To steak a fish, first remove scales, then draw. It will be necessary, also, to cut off fins.

I suppose a sturgeon is the hardest fish to clean. Shark and blowfish are sort of difficult, too, because of their tough skin. Mackerel and blues are a cinch to clean, except that they sometimes come in imposing numbers. They have such small stomachs that drawing is no problem and either very few scales or scales that are easy to remove. The odd fish—permits, for example—will usually be caught in the presence of an old-line charter captain or someone who knows more about deep-sea fish than I do; and I've never known anyone who wasn't willing, when properly approached, to share his knowledge of matters salty.

If a fish can be filleted—and size is the main factor, the fillet-ing of small fish being quite wasteful and impractical—the flavor tends to be more delicate. There are real saltwater types who want their fish cooked bone in because, they say, the bones add to the flavor. I think bone-in cooking makes for a more fishy taste. Skinning the fish or fillet will also make for a more deli-cate flavor. And always, on large fish or small, cut away the thin stomach flaps left when the fish are drawn. In many fish, inside the drawn body cavity, there will be a thin membrane along the backbone that protects blood vessels or nerve sheaths. Removing this membrane and scraping blood and small pieces of loose tissue away will also reduce the strong fishy flavor.

Whole fish, to me, are unappetizing. There are some very fancy ways of cooking fish with head and tail intact; but it always seems a bit barbaric to me, no matter how heavy the table silver may be, to see a whole flounder, for example, lying on a plate with sliced olives where his eyeballs used to be.

BUYING AND STORING FISH

For those who buy fish from time to time, there are some tricks of the trade which are useful in determining how fresh the fish are. First, look at the eyes. In fresh fish, the eyes are full and clear. As fish age, the eyes shrink and sink into the head, becoming cloudy and pinkish. The gills of fresh fish are red and free of slime. Later, they turn grey, brown, and green. The coloring of a fish is helpful in judging freshness, if you know the original markings. The colors fade as the fish grows more stale.

Of course, since fish are seasonal, many fish on the market are frozen. Frozen fish should be kept at or near zero degrees in temperature and should never be refrozen after thawing. A package of frozen fish should not reek to high heaven, and the flesh should be free of any discoloration. There should be a minimum of air space in the package.

In a pamphlet called "Fish and Shellfish for Your Table," the North Carolina Agricultural Extension Service gives some interesting information about how quality is lost in stored fish. Unless properly handled, fish spoil quickly because of bacterial action, oxidation, enzyme action, and dehydration.

Bacterial action can, in part, be controlled by sanitary handling.

Oxidation of the fat or oil in fish, which causes a rancid taste, can be controlled by freezing the fish in water or by wrapping them and placing them in airtight containers before freezing. For small fish, cardboard milk cartons make excellent freezing containers. Fish are packed into the cartons, covered with water, and frozen. A fish frozen in water will keep its fresh taste longer than one that is merely wrapped.

Enzyme action, part of the normal life function of fish, goes on after death but can be controlled by storage temperature.

Dehydration, sometimes called "freezer burn," is simply a loss of moisture, leaving the fish shrunken and dried.

The Agricultural Extension Service gives this guideline as the optimum limits for storing frozen fish: one week in ice cube compartment, one month in across-the-top freezer compartment, six months in separate freezer. Maximum quality in frozen fish is assured by a temperature of zero degrees, but not many home freezers can make the grade there.

The authorities recommend thawing frozen fish in the refrigerator at a temperature of 40 to 45 degrees. This method requires considerable foresight and is completely useless for creatures of impulse who might decide to have fish on the spur of the moment. For the impetuous ones, fish may be thawed in the package under cold running water. This method takes only a half hour or so. Thawing at room temperature, the most used method, is frowned upon because the smaller, thinner parts of the fish thaw immediately and begin to stale while the thick parts are still frozen. I've been thawing fish at room temperature for years, and I didn't know I was doing wrong until I read the aforementioned pamphlet, which goes to show that you learn something new every now and then.

So as not to be brought up for plagiarism, let me say that I am now through paraphrasing the Agricultural Extension Service cooks and will venture back into the uneasy realm of personal opinion and experience.

Frozen fish are a good substitute for no fish at all. Fresh fish are the ideal, and any approach to fresh fish by frozen fish falls just a bit short. Freezing fish completely submerged in water for short periods of time is, in my experience, the best possible way to freeze fish.

There are advocates of freezing fish in the round. It's sort of a lazy man's way of doing things. It saves cleaning the fish, because all you do is rinse them off and freeze them. The day of reckoning comes when you decide to eat the frozen fish, for then the fish must be cleaned. Fish frozen in the round are thawed first, then cleaned as you'd clean a fresh fish. I think there is a stronger taste to fish frozen in the round than to the same kind of fish cleaned before freezing.

Certain fish freeze better than others. Among the fish that seem to freeze well are, fortunately, the big game fish which come in abundance when they come at all—blues, mackerel, billfish, etc. Mackerel seem to hold their flavor best of all. Bluefish will become strong after short periods of freezing, causing people to say, "I don't like bluefish." Fresh, the blue is as good as any of them. He just doesn't take to freezing as well as mackerel but freezes well enough to warrant saving a big blue-fish catch. Mullet frozen for a short period fare rather well but seem to take on a strong, fishy taste over a longer period of time. Trout, with their "weak" flesh, spoil with dismaying quickness. Trout freeze best in fillets submerged in water and should be kept for short periods of time only.

When on a fishing trip, it's a good idea to carry along an ice chest. Ideally, the fisherman concerned primarily with flavor, with eating fish more than with catching them, will draw his fish as they are caught and put them on ice immediately. Some-times this is just not practical; and most fish will keep, except under the hottest, most adverse conditions, for an afternoon, say, while the fishing is still continuing and during the trip back to the dock.

COOKING FISH

Four ounces of fish supply about one-third of the daily adult protein requirement. Fish without sauces and seasonings, except basic ones like salt and butter, are easily digested and will not irritate the tummy. Since today's high-pressure living is wonderfully stomach-irritating, the blandness of fish is some-thing to keep in mind. All fish contain B vitamins and also varying amounts of vitamins A and D. Saltwater fish provide some trace elements that are important to the welfare of the human organism: zinc, cobalt, copper, iron, magnesium, and phosphorus, as well as other minerals that are similar, in general, to those found in beef. In addition, fish are high in iodine, an element needed by the body and present in few other foods.

All of the foregoing has nothing to do with cooking fish but suggests several reasons why it's a good idea to eat fish now and then.

There are really no recipes for basic fish cooking, only methods. A method becomes a recipe when you begin adding ingredients past the simple seasonings. When all the ladies heard that I'd turned my typewriter from the writing of fiction to the preparation of a seafood cookbook, they wanted to feed me their favorite fish dishes and I gained five pounds. I also discovered that the basic ways of cooking fish would take only about two pages to cover. Now you can't very well have a whole section on fish if you say, well, you fry fish in oil after rolling them in meal, can you? But that's exactly the situation. Perhaps I can best illustrate by citing this recipe:

Basic Fish Recipe

2 pounds king, sliced   *Cooking oil or fat*
Milk   *Salt and pepper*
Flour or cornmeal   *Lemon*

Dip slices of fish in salted milk. Roll in seasoned flour or cornmeal. Heat a liberal amount of oil or fat in a heavy skillet. Brown the steaks on one side; turn and brown on other side. Serve with lemon slices. Serves 6.

NOTE: This is a basic method and could be stated as simply as "fry fillets until brown in shallow fat after rolling in mealing mixture." You could use king mackerel, Spanish mackerel, Atlantic mackerel, bluefish, wahoo, or almost any other kind of fish.

Fresh fish may be fried, broiled, steamed, baked, boiled, simmered, or poached.

Frying: Fish is cooked quickly in deep or shallow fat.

Broiling: Fillets or steaks are best for broiling, although small fish may be broiled whole.

Steaming: Fish is suspended above boiling water in a basket or a cheesecloth.

Baking: Whole fish, steaks, or fillets may be baked.

Boiling: Fish is boiled in water. Fine way to cook thick fish steaks.

Simmering: A variation of boiling.

Poaching: A variation of boiling.

You fry fish in hot fat, either shallow or deep, in a deep fryer or in a skillet. All seafood may be skillet-fried or, as the fancy folks say, sautéd. When I use foreign words or phrases, I tend to lisp, feel uncomfortable, and wave my arms. So I prefer the term "fry lightly" to "sauté." Use hot cooking oil, turn frequently, and don't overcook. Butter may be used for light frying; but it's a bit rich for my taste, interfering with the flavor of the meat.

You boil fish. You could have boiled king mackerel, boiled Spanish mackerel, boiled Atlantic mackerel, boiled bluefish, boiled wahoo, etc. Almost any fish can be cooked by any method if an allowance is made for the fat content. You bake fish. When you bake fish, if he's lean, you lard him a bit with butter or bacon. Seasonings may be as basic as lemon juice and butter; or they may be jazzed up with cinnamon, almonds, paprika, celery, thyme, sage, parsley, or almost anything you like.

When fish are cooked in my home—either by the amateur chef or by my capable mate—I find that seasonings are limited to butter, lemon juice, and salt for baked fish and to Dab Sauce for fried fish, and that mealing is done in the most basic manner —rolling water-wetted fish in cornmeal. When having a meal for the family or two or three guests, we shallow-fry fish in small quantities; for large gatherings, we deep-fry outside. It just isn't economical to crank up a deep-fat fryer for a dozen small fish because of the large amount of oil used in deep-fat frying. Although it's possible to use the fat again, there's a storage problem involved.

One general rule holds true of most methods of cooking fish. Do it quickly. Fish sinew is tender. It responds to heat quickly. Overcooking is the most common sin when cooking fish.

Fish are divided loosely into two types, fat and lean. The difference between a fat fish and a lean fish is in the amount of oil. Fat fish have oil throughout the flesh. Lean fish have the oil concentrated in the liver. Thus, lean fish have a drier flesh. In general, lean fish are preferred for frying, steaming, and poaching; fat fish are best for broiling or baking. However, the exception seems to be the rule.

Lean fish include: blackfish, whiting, trout, swordfish, red snapper, drum, mullet, flounder, croaker, and sheephead.

Fat fish include: mackerel, pompano, chicken snapper, barracuda, and sturgeon.

Then, just to show what I mean by saying that the exception seems to be the rule, one educated list of fat and lean fish by a noted authority says that mackerel are fat and that king mackerel are lean. So I list this fat and lean business for what it's worth and will promptly forget it as I pass along recipes gathered from people who have been cooking fish for years.

There are a couple of little tricks of the trade that I might mention:

1. Mackerel may be baked whole with little or no basting.
2. A lean fish may be larded by scoring the skin and inserting bits of salt pork.
3. In frying larger pieces of fish, either whole or filleted, scoring will speed cooking time. (Remember, however, that scoring can be overdone. I've seen cooks score small flounder in cute little square patterns. The finished product looks delicious, all golden brown and cooked up into individual squares, just right to be bite size. However, so much meat is exposed to the hot oil that the fish is cooked to a rather disappointing dryness.)
4. Most cooks seem to agree that salting a fish before cooking improves the flavor.
5. Some spices often used with fish are: basil, marjoram, bay, saffron, and tarragon.
6. A butterfly fillet has nothing to do with insects. It's both sides of a fish, filleted off and connected by the skin of the fish's belly.

Fried Croaker

2 to 4 pan-dressed croakers	Cornmeal or mealing mixture
per person	Salt

Salt the dressed croakers. Roll in cornmeal or mealing mixture. Cook in shallow oil at about 375° for three to five minutes per side, or until fish is brown on the outside and flaky inside.

Steamed Whiting

Whiting fillets   *Salt*

Put fillets in colander or in cheesecloth. Put two inches of water in large kettle; when water begins to boil, suspend fish above water and cover kettle (allowing a vent for the excess steam). Cook about fifteen minutes per pound of fish, or until fish flakes easily. Salt when done. Serve with lemon juice, butter, or a sauce of your choice.

Boiled Mullet

Pan-dressed mullet (small)   *Salt*

Drop mullet into boiling water and cook until fish flakes easily. Salt. Serve with a sauce of your choice.

Baked Mackerel

Spanish or king steaks   *2 tablespoons butter*
Salt and pepper   *1 teaspoon onion, grated*
1 tablespoon lemon juice   *Paprika*

Sprinkle steaks with salt and pepper. Mix lemon juice, butter, and onions and rub into fish. Put fish in greased baking pan. Pour remainder of sauce over fish. Bake at 350° for twenty-five to thirty minutes, or until flaky. Sprinkle with paprika.

Broiled Chicken Snapper

Chicken snapper fillets   *Lemon juice*
Salt and pepper   *Melted butter*

Put fish, skin down, in greased broiler pan. Salt and pepper. Baste with lemon juice and butter. Cook about two inches below broiler unit for ten to fifteen minutes, or until brown. Baste once or twice during cooking. Test thickest part of fish for flakiness. Serve with lemon juice or a sauce of your choice.

Simmered Blackfish

Blackfish, whole or filleted   *2 to 6 peppercorns*
2 slices onion   *1 teaspoon salt*

Put onions, peppercorns, and salt into kettle. Boil for five minutes. Add fish and reduce heat until water is simmering, not boiling. Cook for ten to twenty minutes, or until fish flakes easily. Serve with a sauce of your choice.

Deep-Fat Fried Bluefish

Bluefish, pan-dressed or   *Mealing mixture*
   filleted   *Salt*

Salt bluefish. Meal with deep-fat mealing method. Cook at 375° for three to five minutes, or until brown on the outside and flaky on the inside.

I dimly remember, back when I started this project, stating firmly and emphatically and otherwise redundantly that I was going to emphasize the basic recipes for cooking fish and other seafood. I'm not promising that I won't, if the mood strikes, include a recipe for Fish Chantilly or Fish and Noodles au Gratin. I'm just saying that basic fish cooking does not require much of a recipe. The most delicious fish I've eaten this season were a couple of Atlantic mackerel fillet steaks baked in foil with butter, lemon juice, and salt.

Atlantic Mackerel in Foil

Fillet steaks of Atlantic   Butter
   mackerel   Paprika
Salt   Lemon juice

Salt fish and place on foil. Turn foil up to form a cup. Ladle on soft butter and wrap foil tightly around fish. Bake at 350° about thirty minutes, or until fish flakes easily. Sprinkle with paprika if desired. Squeeze fresh lemon juice on each piece of fish.

Baked King Mackerel with Sauce

King mackerel steaks   Salt and pepper
2 tablespoons butter   ¼ teaspoon Worcestershire
1 tablespoon lemon juice   ½ cup catsup
             Dash of Tabasco

Put steaks on oiled baking dish. Salt and pepper. Bake at 350° for fifteen minutes. Make a sauce of butter, lemon juice, catsup, Worcestershire, and Tabasco and pour over steaks. Bake about ten minutes longer, or until fish flakes easily.

Fresh Salt Mackerel for Breakfast

Thin fillet steaks of mackerel   Pepper
Salt   Butter
            Vinegar

Salt fish heavily and place in refrigerator overnight. To cook, submerge in boiling water and simmer for five to ten minutes, or until fish flakes easily. Make a sauce of melted butter, a touch of vinegar, and pepper. Very good served with grits.

Fish and Chips

Thin fish fillets (about one lb.)	*¼ cup flour*
1 beaten egg	*1 cup fine bread crumbs or*
⅓ cup milk	*other mealing mixture*
1 teaspoon salt	*Pepper to taste*

Potatoes, cut for French fries

Mix egg, flour, milk, salt, and pepper. Cut fillets into sticks and drain on paper towels. Dip in egg-milk mixture and roll in crumbs or mealing mixture. Fry with French fries in shallow or deep fat until golden brown.

Baked Snapper

1 snapper, three to five pounds	*1 tablespoon bacon drippings*
Salt	*1 tablespoon onion, minced*
1 cup bread cubes	*1 teaspoon parsley, minced*
¼ cup milk	*Pepper to taste*

3 slices bacon

Rub inside of fish with salt. Mix bread cubes, milk, bacon drippings, onions, parsley, pepper, and one-half teaspoon salt. Stuff fish with mixture and secure with skewers. Put bacon slices over fish and wrap in foil. Bake at 350° about twenty minutes per pound, or until fish flakes when tested with fork.

Dolphin Fillets

Dolphin, sliced about	*⅓ cup onion, minced*
one-fourth inch thick	*½ teaspoon salt*
3 tablespoons soy sauce	*Pepper to taste*

Mix soy sauce, onions, salt, and pepper in shallow bowl. Dip dolphin slices in mixture and fry lightly in small amount of butter or cooking oil until brown. Do not overcook.

Planked Shad

Shad, about four pounds   *Butter or cooking oil*
Salt   *Large oak plank at least*
Pepper   *two inches thick*

Salt and pepper shad inside and out. Place on greased plank and brush with butter or cooking oil. Bake at 400° about forty minutes, or until tender. Serve on plank or large platter with mashed potatoes arranged around the fish.

NOTE: This one is something of a tradition. Families used to keep the shad plank from season to season. The theory is that the plank absorbs most of the oils from the fish as it is baked. Almost any large fish can be planked. If the fish is in the "lean" category, baste frequently with butter or oil. A large, oven-proof platter may be substituted for the plank. Shad roe may be served with planked shad.

Limed Mullet

2 pounds mullet fillets   *Dash pepper*
¼ cup lime juice, preferably   *3 tablespoons butter*
*   fresh*   *Paprika*
1 teaspoon salt   *Lime wedges*

In shallow dish, sprinkle fish with salt and pepper and, lightly, with lime juice. Let stand for thirty minutes, turning once and sprinkling other side with same ingredients. Mix remaining lime juice with butter. Put fish in broiler pan and baste with butter and lime juice. Cook under broiler for eight to ten minutes, or until flaky. Sprinkle with paprika. Serve with lime wedges.

Baked Mullet with Cheese

1 *mullet, large*	1 *tsp. dry mustard (optional)*
2 *or 3 slices soft, yellow cheese*	¼ *teaspoon Worcestershire*
1 *small onion, chopped*	1 *teaspoon salt*
1 *cup milk*	*Pepper to taste*

Put onions and a slice of cheese inside fish. Mix milk, mustard, Worcestershire, salt, and pepper. Pour over fish in baking pan and arrange cheese slices on top. Bake at 400° for twenty-five to thirty minutes.

Baked Grouper

2 *lbs. grouper steaks or fillets*	1 *teaspoon prepared mustard*
1 *lemon, sliced*	¼ *teaspoon paprika*
1 *onion, sliced*	*Salt*
1 *cup sour cream*	*Pepper*

Arrange lemon and onion slices in greased baking dish and sprinkle with salt and pepper. Add fillets and bake, covered or wrapped in foil, at 400° about twenty minutes, or until fish flakes easily. Make a sauce of cream, one-half teaspoon salt, mustard, and paprika. Spread sauce on fish and broil three inches below heat until brown.

Stuffed Flounder

Flounder (about one pound)	2 *teaspoons lemon juice*
¼ *pound crab meat*	*Mealing mixture*
Salt and pepper	

Dress flounder by scaling and cutting off head. Draw intestines through opening at head. Sprinkle with salt and pepper and cut pocket under skin on thick side of flounder. Mix crab meat, lemon juice, salt, and pepper and stuff into opening. Roll fish in mealing mixture. Fry in light oil at 375° for five to ten minutes per side, or until fish is flaky.

Mushroom-Stuffed Flounder

Flounder, about two pounds
1 can mushrooms, chopped
1/3 cup butter
1 onion, chopped

1/2 cup bread crumbs
1/4 cup celery, chopped
1 tablespoon parsley, minced
Salt and pepper

Cook onions in butter until tender. Add mushrooms and cook for five minutes. Remove from heat. Add bread crumbs, celery, parsley, salt, and pepper. Mix. Cut pocket under skin of flounder on thick side and stuff in mixture. Secure opening with skewers. Bake in greased pan at 400° for twenty to thirty minutes, or until fish flakes easily.

Blackfish and Pineapple

2 pounds blackfish fillets
1/2 cup pineapple juice

1 tablespoon butter
1 teaspoon salt

Pepper to taste

Melt butter in pineapple juice. Add salt and pepper and pour over fish in shallow dish. Let stand for thirty minutes, turning once. Broil for four to six minutes and baste. Turn, baste, and broil for four to six minutes longer, or until fish is flaky.

Curried Fish

6 *small fillets of any fish*　　　½ *teaspoon sugar*
4 *large tomatoes*　　　　　　　*Salt and pepper*
1 *onion*　　　　　　　　　　　*Flour*
1½ *teaspoons curry powder*　　　¼ *cup cream*

Peel and chop tomatoes and onion. Cook together over low heat for thirty to forty minutes, or until thick. Add curry powder, sugar, one-half teaspoon salt, and pepper. Meal fillets in flour and fry in light oil or butter until brown. Season with salt and pepper and place on platter. Add cream to tomato-onion mixture and bring to boil. Pour over fish and serve while hot.

Queen of the Sea–The Oyster

THE EARLIEST KNOWN GOURMETS TO VISIT THE SOUTHEASTERN
North Carolina coast were members of an obscure Indian tribe
of dubious origin. Little is known about the coastal tribes, but
local residents espouse the theory that the Indians spent all
of their time either making or breaking fired clay pottery. All

along the Lower Cape Fear River, potsherds abound. Rarely can you dig a hole in the ground without finding a piece of fired clay pottery.

However, there is, on the sandy stretch of Oak Island, conclusive proof that the early Indians had time for at least one activity other than making pottery.

They ate oysters.

Remnants of ancient oyster feasts are everywhere. There are no impressive, huge mounds of discarded oyster shells as there are in some coastal areas. Our Indians were, apparently, a footloose lot, moving often, never staying in one place long enough to build more than a six-inch layer of shells.

But those early North Carolinians loved their oysters. How much they loved the queen of all seafoods is demonstrated by early, unauthenticated reports by historians and observers regarding Indians, oysters, and a branch of the holly family known as yaupon. (Pronounced *yaw'-pon* according to my battered desk dictionary, *you'-pon'* according to the latest Webster's Unabridged, and *yo'-pon* in local usage. And to compound the confusion, some people misspell it as youpon.)

Yaupon is not only sort of multidextrous in spelling and pronunciation; it is a bush of confused legend. There is one story which says that yaupon was used by early settlers along the Cape Fear as a substitute for tea. There is an equally convincing tradition that the Indians used yaupon tea as an emetic. Lending credence to the latter is the Latin name of yaupon, *Ilex vomitoria*, which presents a vivid picture, even to a nonlinguist.

Oysters and a black drink made of yaupon were the only ingredients of the early Indian seafood feasts along the Cape Fear. I do not recommend the Indian Oyster Feast. It is one of the few recipes in the book that I have not tried, and I hereby absolve myself from liability in the event some adventurer would like to verify his anthropological research by experiment.

Indian Oysters with Yaupon Tea

Yaupon leaves, freshly gathered, washed
Oysters, gathered fresh from the muddy waters of a tidal
creek or river

Boil yaupon leaves in brackish water, using a fired clay pot over an open fire. Serve in fired clay drinking cups. Break oysters open with a rock or a flint knife. Eat raw; drink juices. When totally glutted with oysters, drink yaupon tea. Vomit to empty stomach. Glut on oysters again. (May be repeated as long as you can stand it.)

Long before the coastal Indians proved their love for oysters, the Chinese were cultivating oysters artificially. The Romans, too, farmed oysters. Much has been written in speculation about the first man to eat an oyster. Looking at an oyster for the first time, one agrees that this pioneer was a desperate man; but he was rewarded by a flavor unlike that of anything else on earth.

What is it that gives the oyster its flavor? Paramyosin, a muscle protein that is found only in bivalves, could have an effect on the taste. The pleasant saltiness of an oyster is probably accounted for by the fact that an adult specimen of *O. virginica*, the common eastern oyster, can pump as much as thirty-seven quarts of sea water through its system during a pleasant, summer hour. Winter oysters are probably less salty in taste because the oyster hibernates, by closing its shell, when the water temperature drops to about forty-three degrees.

Another contributing factor to the taste of an oyster is locale. When someone says he favors the taste of oysters from a particular area, there is foundation to his contention that some oysters are better than others. Since it is about three-quarters water, the oyster takes on the mineral characteristics of the water that it pumps through its system. For example, in areas where there is considerable industrial waste, an oyster can absorb so much copper that it turns green. The ability of the oyster to utilize the contents of the surrounding water accounts for many small, stenciled signs seen along the Cape Fear River:

CLOSED SHELLFISH AREA

A funny little bacterium, fortunately harmless, which is flourishing at this moment in the intestines of all of us, serves as a guide for posting those signs. When the bacterium level of the oyster reaches a specified point, up go the signs; for the presence of the harmless germs indicates the presence, or the possible presence, of other germs that are not harmless.

Directly behind my home on Oak Island, the marshes are cut by a multitude of tidal creeks. Lush, plump oysters love it there. Ungathered, they grow in the creek below the bank in my back yard, absorbing the riches floated down to them by upstream cities in the form of untreated sewage. An oyster taken from such polluted waters can carry, along with a deceptively good flavor, various undesirable microbes which lead to unpleasant effects on the human organism.

In short, don't take oysters from polluted waters. If in doubt about an oyster, don't eat it. The effects of eating polluted oysters can range from nothing—leading some skeptics to ignore the posted signs—to immediate and severe vomiting, or even to long-range, serious disease.

When buying oysters, one need not worry too much about

pollution, unless the purchase is made from the friendly, neighborhood oyster peddler. In that case, it's a good idea to know your man—and thus know your oysters—for, although the gathering of oysters is controlled by state authorities, not even the use of sea planes and boats can ensure that no one will gather bad oysters.

Fresh oysters, whether self-gathered or bought in the shell, should be tightly closed or should close when tapped. "Fresh" can mean still dripping with salt water or a couple of days out of the water, depending on temperature and handling. One species of oyster can survive for over ninety days out of water if kept at a temperature a few degrees above freezing, unless rough handling causes the muscles of the oyster to relax, thus opening the valves and losing the water held inside the shell. So, yesterday's oysters are "fresh" as long as they are still alive.

Shucked oysters should be plump and creamy colored and should smell fresh, like salt air and marsh. The liquid of the oyster should be slightly milky in color, and the odor should be slight, not overpowering. The oyster may have a black, tan, or brown fringe around the edge.

GATHERING OYSTERS

By far the simplest method of gathering oysters is to buy a can of fresh, shucked oysters at the meat or seafood counter of the local supermarket. One of the more pleasurable ways of taking oysters involves immersion in salt water. When conservation laws allow, I like to take to a shallow tidal creek, in an unpolluted area and at low tide, wearing a swim suit and pushing before me a bushel basket floating in the ring of an inflated inner tube. Oysters may be located by wading along until the naked toe encounters a single oyster or a clump. Needless to say, the toe should be used gingerly, since oyster shells, both dead and alive, are considerably tougher than human skin.

In deeper waters, oyster tongs or rakes may be used. An oyster rake may be the garden rake doing double duty. Tongs are usually custom-built, with handles ten or more feet long mounted on opposing, scissorlike rakes which dig under the oysters and lift them. Oyster tonging is backbreaking work. Because it requires a boat and a set of shoulder muscles used to the task, tonging is usually reserved for the professional oysterman.

In some coastal areas oyster growers, following the pattern set by the Chinese long before the Christian era, lease suitable bottoms from the state and cultivate oysters by artificial methods. Gathering oysters from a commercial oyster farm is comparable to stealing watermelons and is definitely not recommended.

To find oysters requires some knowledge of the area. Beachgoers who frequent the same shore community year after year discover the best oyster grounds by experiment or by asking some friendly native. Fortunately, the oyster is one of the most common bivalves, and there are usually enough to go around. Natives may not be willing to tell where the big, single oysters grow best; but they will usually point out an area where clump oysters may be found. As far as taste is concerned, the small oysters are as good as the large ones. Smaller oysters just require more work for the same amount of return.

SHUCKING OYSTERS

When freshly gathered oysters are safely at home, the first necessity is washing. Oysters are likely to have a liberal sampling of their native mud or sand clinging to their shells, and opening an unwashed oyster mixes mud and grit with the shucked meat.

Oysters that have been removed from muddy bottoms should be scrubbed with a stiff bristle brush until all mud and grit is gone. Oysters from hard or sandy bottoms may be cleaned with running water.

There are those who say—Pappy Stubbs of Southport being one of them—that an oyster doesn't taste right unless you eat a little mud with it, but I am forced to disagree and advise thorough washing.

Shucking an oyster, for a novice, can be like pushing a hand into a stack of used razor blades. A heavy pair of work gloves is advisable, and the proper oyster knife is a must. Experts can open an oyster with a variety of instruments ranging from a pocket knife to a screwdriver, but the safest and most efficient instrument is a special knife with a short, stiff blade and a large wooden handle. My favorite oyster knife has an ovate guard plate between the blade and the handle to prevent the oyster shell from cutting the hand in case of a slip.

An oyster is attached to its shell by two powerful muscles. A force of about thirty pounds is needed to tear the muscle of an adult American oyster. When attacking an oyster, it is best to start from the narrow, or dorsal, end. The hinge of the two shells is located there, and the hinge offers the easiest point of access. Hold the oyster firmly in your left hand, with its dorsal end toward your body. Steady your hand on a table top and, with the other hand, push the point of the oyster knife into the hinge of the oyster, applying steady pressure and twisting the knife. This slow, steady, twisting pressure will penetrate the hinge, allowing the stiff knife blade to pry the two shells apart. When the knife has made entry into the oyster's shell, a slicing motion will cut on one side the muscle that holds the oyster to the shell.

Let me emphasize the necessity of having both hands braced against a slip. Careless jabbing at an oyster can result in plunging the knife hand against the oyster's sharp shell or in puncturing with the knife the hand holding the oyster.

In taking oysters from nature, the gathering is only the beginning. Cleaning and shucking oysters requires time and effort, and the gathering is easier than the preparation. If you, as a beginner with oysters, find a spot where the gathering is easy, don't overdo it. Start with collecting half a bushel; then work up. Shucking a bushel of oysters can be a day's work for one who isn't familiar with the technique. If the oyster were not so delicious, it wouldn't be worth the effort.

Oysters are shucked for frying, for stewing, and for making cocktails. For roasting or steaming, it is necessary only to scrub the oyster.

One other comment on oyster shucking: I have talked with people who say that they facilitate shucking by putting fresh oysters into the freezer for a couple of hours. It is said that freezing causes the shells to pop open. If this method is tried, care must be taken not to leave the oysters in the freezer too long. Overfreezing dries out the natural liquid of the oyster, and this is a vital part of many oyster dishes.

NOW, LET'S EAT

To the die-hard seafood lover, the flavor of a raw oyster is tops in eating. I know fishermen who never take lunch on a fishing trip. When hungry, they just pull alongside an oyster bed, take out their trusty pocket knives, and lunch is served.

The basic oyster cocktail is the fisherman's lunch moved onto the patio:

Basic Oyster Cocktail

Shucked oysters

Serve chilled oysters in a container compatible with table setting. That's all.

However, an oyster cocktail can be much more decorative and more complex:

More Complicated Oyster Cocktail

Shucked oysters   *Cocktail sauce*
Lettuce   *Lemon wedges*

Drain oysters on paper towel or in colander. Serve in lettuce cups on salad plates or on lettuce in sherbet glasses.

Oyster Cocktail with Dab Sauce

Shucked oysters   *Worcestershire*
Catsup   *Tabasco*

Pour a couple of dabs of catsup into an individual container. Add a dash of Worcestershire and a dash of Tabasco to taste. Pour over oysters or give each person a container so that he can dip his own oysters into sauce.

Oysters on the Half Shell

Oysters

Shuck scrubbed oysters, cutting muscles on both sides of shell, but leaving oysters on one half shell. Serve with shells resting in cracked ice.

It's easy to see that Oysters on the Half Shell is just a variation on the Basic Oyster Cocktail. Half-shell oysters may be served on individual plates at a formal dinner or may be placed around a bowl of cocktail sauce for snacks.

OYSTER ROAST

The Oyster Roast is a tradition in coastal Carolina. The ease of preparing roasted oysters recommends the method to those who like to eat but don't like to cook. Equipment can range from an elaborate back-yard barbecue pit to a bed of coals on a moonlit strand. Only a few things are required for an Oyster Roast: a fire; a means of supporting the oysters over the coals; perhaps a dampened cloth to cover the oysters and keep the moisture in; and fresh, washed oysters.

Special oyster-roasting pits utilize a flat piece of metal or a screen or a grill over a firebed. Ordinary hamburger grills may be used quite successfully by covering the grill with foil to equalize the heat under the oysters and to prevent the water used to dampen the cloth from dripping onto the fire. In the open, oysters may be cooked directly in a bed of coals, then rinsed in the surf to remove the ashes before opening. Any piece of metal, such as a flattened gallon can, may be placed on a bed of coals and used as a roaster. Salt water may be used to dampen the cover cloth.

Oysters are heated, with or without dampening, until the muscles relax, allowing the shells to open. Roasted oysters come in varying degrees of rawness. If the good flavor of raw oysters is prized, oysters are roasted only until the shells begin to open. Longer roasting will result in a fully cooked oyster, but one that will be dried of its natural juices. One method of timing the roasting of oysters is to cover the cooking shells with a heavy, wet cloth—anything from a gunnysack to a towel. When the cloth is dried by the heat, the oysters are ready. Longer roasting will require redampening the cloth.

The chief advantage of roasting oysters, for those who want to retain the basic, raw flavor, is that heat makes the shells pop open or, at least, facilitates their opening.

As with all seafood, sauce is a matter of individual taste with roasted oysters. Roasted oysters may be dipped in melted butter; garnished with lemon; flavored with a favorite sauce, if only a touch of Tabasco; or eaten as they come from the shell.

Indoor Oyster Roast

Scrubbed oysters   *Melted butter*

Place oysters on baking sheet and roast in 450° oven about fifteen minutes, or until shells begin to pop open. As oysters roast, melt butter. Serve oysters on half shell with melted butter.

No specific quantity of oysters is called for in the above recipe because it is impossible to predict how many oysters an individual will eat. If the main and only course is roasted oysters, a couple of hungry men can demolish a bushel of oysters. If the roasted oysters are being used as an appetizer, six large oysters per person is a good serving. Since oysters are mostly water and about one-tenth protein, the calorie count is pleasingly low. One serving of six large, raw oysters contains only sixty calories.

STEAMED OYSTERS

Steaming, like roasting, preserves the basic flavor of the oyster. Any large container may be used. Place scrubbed oysters in the container, pour in enough water to cover the bottom of the container, and cover oysters with a thoroughly wetted cloth.

Cook over medium heat until the water has steamed away or until the oysters begin to pop open. It may be necessary to add more water if steaming stops before the shells begin to open.

A variation on the above method is to put a wet cloth in the bottom of the container, place the oysters on the cloth, and cover with a second wet cloth. Cook as above, adding water as necessary to continue the steaming process.

Eating steamed or roasted oysters is rather messy, unless the oysters are pre-opened and served on the half shell as an appetizer. If the main course is oysters, it's best to serve them outside or on the porch or patio. A properly prepared oyster is going to drip fluid when opened, so quantities of newspaper or towels may be used to protect clothing, tables, and floors. Both steamed and roasted oysters are best eaten while hot. Sauce is a matter of taste. Saltine crackers go well with oysters.

Fried Oysters

Shucked oysters   *Mealing mixture*

Drain oysters on paper towels. Dip in mealing mixture and fry in deep fat at 375° for no more than five minutes.

Oyster Stew

1 *pint shucked oysters*   ½ *teaspoon salt*
1 *quart milk*   1 *tablespoon butter*
Black pepper

Put milk, salt, and butter in saucepan and heat to scalding. Add oysters with their natural juices. Pepper to taste. Simmer about five minutes, or until flavor of oysters has permeated milk. Overcooking makes the oysters tough.

NOTE: For more liberal portions with the same number of oysters, as much as two quarts of milk may be used.

Oyster stew prepared as above keeps the natural flavor of the oyster. The secret to good oyster stew is: *Do not overcook.* The oysters floating in the stew should be juicy inside.

I realize, however, that there are some poor souls who don't like the taste of a raw oyster. For such, I present the following— a stew with a different, more fully cooked taste and with more body in the stock:

Precooked Oyster Stew

1 *pint shucked oysters*	½ *teaspoon salt*
2 *tablespoons flour*	2 *tablespoons water*
Black pepper	1 *quart milk*
	2 *tablespoons butter*

Blend flour, pepper, salt, and water into a smooth paste. Stir paste into oysters with their liquid. Simmer in saucepan over low heat until the edges of the oysters begin to curl, five minutes or more. Pour in milk, which has been heated to scalding. Remove pan from heat and let stand for fifteen minutes. Add butter. Reheat and serve.

There are many other ways of preparing oysters, usually involving seasonings and additions that result in dishes in which the oyster is only a hidden flavor. I will offer only a few of such carefully calibrated oyster side dishes.

Oysters au Gratin

1 *pint shucked oysters*	1 *teaspoon prepared mustard*
6 *slices buttered toast*	*(optional)*
2 *beaten eggs*	½ *teaspoon paprika (optional)*
1 *teaspoon salt*	½ *cup milk*

1 *cup mild cheese, grated*

Trim crusts from toast and cut into quarters. Combine eggs, seasonings, and milk. Put a layer of toast in casserole dish, cover with oysters, and sprinkle with cheese. Repeat layers, topping last layer with cheese. Pour milk-egg mixture over and sprinkle with cheese. Place dish in pan of hot water and bake at 350° for at least thirty minutes, or until brown.

Scalloped Oysters

1 *pint shucked oysters*	*Black pepper to taste*
2 *cups cracker crumbs*	½ *cup melted butter*
½ *teaspoon salt*	*Dash Worcestershire*

1 *cup milk*

Drain oysters on paper towels or in colander. Combine cracker crumbs, salt, pepper, and butter. Place a third of mixture in casserole and cover with oysters. Repeat layers. Add Worcestershire to milk and pour over layered mixture. Bake at 350° about thirty minutes, or until brown.

Oysters with Noodles

1 *pint shucked oysters*	½ *green pepper, chopped*
3 *tablespoons butter*	½ *teaspoon salt*
3 *tablespoons flour*	*Black pepper to taste*
1½ *cups milk*	½ *cup bread crumbs*
1½ *cups cooked noodles*	2 *tablespoons butter*

Drain oysters on paper towels or in colander. Make a white sauce by melting three tablespoons butter in top of double boiler, blending in flour, and adding milk. Cook until thick, stirring constantly. Layer noodles in buttered casserole, with layer of oysters on top. Sprinkle with green pepper, salt, and black pepper. Repeat layers. Pour white sauce over contents of casserole and cover with buttered bread crumbs. Bake at 350° about thirty minutes, or until brown.

Creamed Oysters

1 *pint shucked oysters*	3 *cups milk*
½ *cup butter*	1 *teaspoon salt*
½ *cup flour*	*Black pepper*

Simmer oysters in their juice about five minutes, or until edges begin to curl. Drain off liquid. Melt butter in top of double boiler, blend in flour, add milk, and cook over medium heat until mixture thickens, stirring constantly. Add oysters and seasonings. Heat and serve on toast.

Deviled Oysters

1 *quart oysters*	2 *tablespoons parsley, chopped*
½ *cup onion, chopped*	2 *tablespoons catsup*
2 *tablespoons cooking oil*	*Juice of small lemon*
1 *cup cracker crumbs*	*Dash Tabasco*
½ *cup celery, chopped*	*Salt and pepper*
2 *tablespoons Worcestershire*	*Butter*
½ *cup dry bread crumbs*	

Brown onions in cooking oil. In another container, heat oysters in their own liquid until edges curl. Remove oysters, and to the liquid add onions and all ingredients except butter and bread crumbs. Add oysters and put into buttered baking dish. Sprinkle with bread crumbs, dot with butter, and bake at 425° for fifteen to twenty minutes, or until oysters are sizzling but not cooked dry.

Oyster Cocktail with Cucumbers

Oysters   *Sliced cucumbers*
Dab Sauce made to taste with catsup, Worcestershire, and Tabasco

Heat oysters in their liquid until edges curl. Drain liquid off and let oysters cool. Reduce liquid by boiling over high heat until very little remains. Mix with Dab Sauce. Layer oysters and cucumbers in cocktail or sherbet glass and pour sauce on top. For chilled cocktail, cool sauce before adding to oysters and cucumbers.

OYSTER FACTS THAT MAY OR MAY NOT BOGGLE THE SENSES

The oyster is a mixed-up mollusk of the class Bivalvia (or Lamellibranchia or Pelecypoda). The Latin name refers to the fact that the oyster has two shells. The oyster lives in shallow coastal waters between latitudes 64° N. and 44° S. It has been said that the oyster can't have much fun because it is rooted to a shell bed, but there is a time in the career of the oyster when it is a free-swimming, footloose youngster. The oyster larva has a foot, much like that of a traveling mollusk, which allows it to swim and crawl until it finds a home and attaches itself to some object permanently.

And as far as having fun is concerned, some species of oyster are both male and female, producing both eggs and sperm in the same shell. Just what does go on in that shell? Other species change sex occasionally as an outlet from boredom. In the common eastern oyster, most youngsters start life as males and change their sex toward the end of their first year.

The old saw about oysters not being fit to eat in the R-less months may have come into being because the increased amount of water being pumped through their systems makes them seem more watery in summer and because they spoil more rapidly in hot weather. There is also common sense in not taking oysters during the warm months, for that is when they spawn. In my neighborhood, Davis Creek and Lockwood Folly oysters seem to be plumper, creamier, and tastier in the summer; and it's also much more pleasant to gather oysters in warm weather. In years past, individuals have been allowed to take limited amounts of summer oysters for personal use. Since conservation rules change from time to time, check with local authorities or with local residents who are up-to-date on regulations before gathering oysters.

Oysters eat minute algae and other microorganisms and are eaten by oyster drills, starfish, raccoons, and people. If all the empty oyster shells of all the oysters ever eaten by the human race were placed end to end, that would be one heck of a lot of oyster shells.

A Quahog by Any Other
Name–The Clam

BLAME IT ON A TRIBE OF EASTERN INDIANS, THE ALGONQUIAN
bunch. The problem was, they didn't know a clam when they
saw one. Thus, quahog. That's the hard-shelled, tough, difficult-
to-open clam of the East Coast which is the basic ingredient

for all the clam chowder south of Chesapeake Bay—where they have another kind of clam called the soft-shell or long-necked clam. Varley Lang, in a very interesting book called *Follow the Water*, covers soft-shell clams and Chesapeake Bay living. I rather envy those who live in soft-shell country because hard-shell clams are a bear to open. And once you get the cotton-pickin' things open, they're as tough as whitleather and, in most cases, have to be ground.

But if all this sounds as if I'm anti-clam, I'm not. Clams have many advantages, not the least of which is their accessibility. Almost any tidewater creek or sand flat will yield clams. Clams lie in the sand close to the surface and in a vertical position. In clear water, if the clam is undisturbed, it is possible to see the siphon which the clam extends above the sand to gather food from the water. It's customary, when gathering clams, to carry an oyster knife so that the first small clam to be taken may be eaten raw. This assures good luck for the rest of the day.

The first time I went clam gathering was after Hazel, the big hurricane of 1954. Along a large stretch of coast, time is divided into two eras—before Hazel and after Hazel. The hurricane devastated the beaches below the Cape Fear and wiped out a friend who had an establishment on Holden's Beach. The friend, a genial gentleman with a withered arm and a sense of humor, set up shop on Emerald Isle Beach, which was in a pioneering stage at that time. Hurricanes seemed to follow our friend, for next year there were Connie, Diane, and Ione; but they didn't make the killer-hurricane class, as did Hazel.

In the mid-fifties there were a motel, a fishing pier, and a couple of cottages on Emerald Isle Beach. The strand was un-spoiled, with huge sand dunes lining the front. Behind, Bogue Sound made an excellent play area for small children, with which we were then blessed. I began to appreciate the sea and its products during the weekends we spent on Emerald Isle. For example, I've been spoiled ever since about floundering. We used to go out on just about any tide and find flounder to gig in Bogue Sound. I had my first "conch" chowder, made from whelks taken alive while we were wading in the sound; and our friend Nick taught us how to get clams with nothing more than our toes.

We had decided to try a clambake, northern style, after reading about it in some book written by a Yankee who neglected to go into detail about the type of clams or the type of seaweed. All we needed was clams, so Nick told us to go out into the sound and wade around and feel for the clams with our toes. We did. We saw a couple of people with long rakes working away, burdened down with buckets and other paraphernalia. We didn't know what they were after, but we were after clams; and we began to dig in the sand with our toes, striking a sharp-edged, broken shell now and then and wincing. But we found clams, and we went back to the motel with a toy float full of them.

The next step was to find some rocks to heat in the fire. Rocks are rather scarce along the beach, but we found some left over from a building project. Then there was the task of gathering seaweed from the sound. We dug a hole in the wet sand, built a fire, let it burn down to embers, put in the rocks and let them become hot, covered the rocks with wet seaweed, and put in a layer of clams and another layer of seaweed. It worked wonderfully. The clams steamed and opened and smelled fine. The only problem was that Bogue Sound seaweed is probably the sandiest seaweed in the Western world. A small amount of sand at a cookout is tolerable. The quantity of sand we found in our clams drove us back into the motel for a very unseafoodlike hamburger.

But you can, by golly, get clams with no other weapon than your toes. In shallow water, you can crawl and run your fingers through the sand. It's tough on fingernails; and now and then you hit a piece of broken shell, and it smarts a bit. If the water is too deep to crawl, or if I'm working an exposed sand flat that gets rather solid when out of the water, I use a regular garden rake.

In my part of saltwater country, there has been a run on clams in the last couple of years. My favorite creek has been almost clammed out. Some of the creek has been seeded and is closed to clamming. That's something to watch for: small signs, usually placed about a half mile across the creek so that you either have to swim a good distance to read them or carry a set of binoculars, saying CLOSED TO CLAMMING. SHELLS SEEDED. These signs indicate that the oyster and clam crop of the future is growing there; and with the increased population of the beach areas, conservation is a must. It takes almost five years to grow a clam three inches in size.

Interestingly enough, one authority on clams states that large clams are no good for breeding purposes and that it is the medium-sized clams that spawn. So leaving the huge clams is not particularly good conservation; it's just good policy, for the larger a clam is, the tougher he is. An old granddaddy four or five inches across just about has to be opened with a sledge hammer and is so tough that he might shatter the meat grinder going through.

There are about fifteen thousand kinds of clams, and many of them are edible. The surf clam, for example, is an important commercial species and is canned in large quantities. The jack-knife, or broad razor clam, is important along the West Coast. I mention this because there is a species of razor clam along the East Coast, small in our area and difficult to find alive, but, I'm told, very delicious and tender. I'm going to give the razor clam a try if I ever find it in sufficient quantities while on a clam-digging expedition.

Along with the common clam on the East Coast, one often finds a small, white, ribbed clam of about one to one and a half inches in size. This type of clam, called Venus by some and mistakenly called cherrystone by others, is dark and unappetizing. I've cooked and eaten the elegant Sunray Venus clam and the pretty calico clam, but I've never had the nerve to tackle the little Venus.

Cherrystone clams—and I use the term in the recognized sense, meaning small quahogs—are eaten raw and share the dubious distinction of being, along with the oyster, the only animal customarily eaten alive by us civilized Americans. Clams are also eaten alive by blue crabs, horseshoe crabs, clam borers, and certain species of ray. Easily accessible and almost as im-mobile as the oyster, a clam has a life, I should say, filled with tribulations.

Clams, like oysters, can be dangerous if taken from polluted waters. When gathering clams, know your water and look out for the CLOSED SHELLFISH AREA signs.

The quahog is about the only clam that keeps well. He's able to close his shell tightly and retain his water, so he'll keep for weeks under refrigeration. A fresh clam is so tightly closed that it takes might and main to get him open. If a clam gives up too easily, beware. Don't use a clam with a broken shell which has been out of the water for any length of time.

GETTING A CLAM OPEN

Unless you relish sand with your food, wash clams under running water, brushing with a bristle brush. Small clams, like oysters, may be opened with any tool ranging from a screwdriver to a butcher knife. By far the best implement is the stiff, short-bladed oyster knife with the ovate guard between blade and hilt to protect the hand.

Clams are hinged with a tough muscle located on the thick side. Attack the clam on the thick side, in the shiny black strip between the two shell halves. On clams up to about two inches in size, use the oyster knife. Hold the clam firmly, with both hands braced on a solid surface if possible. With a twisting, pushing motion, insert the tip of the knife blade between the shells at the hinge, pry the shells apart, slip the knife further in, and cut the strong holding muscle.

For clams above two inches in size, I advise other methods of opening. One way is freezing, which expands the liquid inside and forces the shells apart. All of the clam juice is preserved when this method is used. Another way is steaming. Put washed clams in a container having a lid. Put a small amount of water in the container and heat until steam causes the clams to open slightly. The disadvantage of steaming is that all or most of the clam liquor is lost.

Large clams to be used in chowder may be opened with a large, strong knife and a wooden mallet. This method should not be used by the faint-hearted because of the ever-present danger to the digits of the clam opener. Put the clam on a chopping board, thick side down, in a vertical position. Insert the sharp side of a butcher knife blade into the tiny space between the closed shells on the slender side of the clam. Tap the knife with a wooden mallet to force the blade into the shell from the narrow side. *Do not try to hold clam with free hand.* When the knife is forced into the shell it slices the main body of the clam, but that doesn't really matter, since the clams are to be ground for chowder anyway.

The problem of sand and shell particles in the juice, which is used in many recipes, can be solved by straining the liquid through several thicknesses of cheesecloth. In using large clams for chowder, it is advisable to cut out the dark stomach area of the clam, for it usually contains a deposit of sand and grit. This is quite easy to accomplish when frozen clams are used.

By far the most common use of the quahog is in a chowder, of which there are many variations. Clam fritters are also a favorite. Small, tender clams may be fried; but they are not as tender as the northern soft-shell clam, which is more like an oyster in consistency.

Cherrystone Clams on the Half Shell
Small Clams

Wash clams. Open with oyster knife. Cut clam free of both halves of shell. Put on one shell and serve, chilled, with a sauce of your choice.

Cherrystone Clam Cocktail
Small Clams

Open small quahogs after washing thoroughly. Drain on paper towels. Serve in nest of lettuce in sherbet glass. May be topped with a sauce of your choice or with a Dab Sauce of catsup, Tabasco, and Worcestershire.

Fried Cherrystone Clams
Small clams   *Mealing mixture*
                          Salt and pepper

Open clams and drain on paper towels. Roll in mealing mixture, into which salt and pepper have been sprinkled. May be deep fried at 375° or fried in small amount of fat in frying pan until brown.

Roasted Clams on the Half Shell

Clams under two inches in size	Catsup
	Worcestershire
Bacon, cut into one-inch squares	Tabasco
	Liquid Smoke
Clam liquor	

Pry clams open, cut loose from shells, and leave on half shell. Make sauce with catsup, dash of Worcestershire, dash of Tabasco, and tiny dash of Liquid Smoke. Dilute about half with clam liquor and pour into half shell over clam. Put bacon square on top and broil in oven until bacon is done but not brown.

Creamed Clams on Toast

2 to 3 cups ground or chopped clams	¼ teaspoon pepper
	2 cups milk
6 tablespoons butter	½ cup celery, cooked and chopped
8 tablespoons flour	
1 teaspoon salt	1 tablespoon parsley, chopped
Salt and pepper to taste	

Make a white sauce by melting butter and adding flour, salt, and pepper. Stir until well mixed. Remove from heat and stir in milk. Cook, while stirring, until smooth. Add clams, celery, parsley, and seasonings. Heat to boiling. Serve on toast.

Clam Fritters

1

2 *cups ground or chopped* *clams*	¼ *teaspoon pepper*
1 *cup flour*	*Clam liquor*
1 *teaspoon salt*	*Milk*
	2 *beaten eggs*

Mix flour, salt, and pepper. To clam liquor, add enough milk to make one cup of liquid. Stir into flour. Add eggs and clams. Batter should be of the consistency of pancake batter. Fry on hot griddle or skillet in small amount of cooking oil or fat at sizzling temperature until brown.

2

2 *cups ground or chopped* *clams*	½ *teaspoon salt*
2 *cups flour*	*Pepper to taste*
1 *teaspoon baking powder*	½ *cup clam liquor*
	1 *cup milk*
2 *beaten eggs*	

Mix dry ingredients. Add liquid ingredients and stir. Fold in clams. Spoon into deep fat and cook at 375° until brown.

3

2 *cups ground or chopped* *clams*	½ *teaspoon salt*
1 *cup pancake flour*	1 *beaten egg*
	Milk

Mix flour, salt, and egg with milk to consistency of pancake batter. Stir in clams. Fry on hot griddle until brown.

Clambread

1 to 2 cups ground clams
Cornbread batter (See chapter on breads or use commercial
cornbread mix)

Add ground clams to cornbread batter or cornbread mix and
bake as directed until brown.

Clam Chowder

Nothing gives the creative cook a greater opportunity for
freedom of expression than clam chowder, for making a good
chowder is mostly putting in some of this and some of that—a
matter of feel and experience. And most chowders, like a good
stew, improve with repeated cookings or heatings. There's one
recipe, in fact, that calls for a cooling-off period of from twelve
to twenty-four hours before reheating and eating.

If the potent flavor of cooked clams is too strong, it can be
altered with a galaxy of additives and with every strong flavoring agent from onions to oregano. The clam's flavor will withstand garlic and thyme, or carrots and onions and potatoes, or
thickening agents such as flour and meal. The hearty clam will
withstand almost any insult and come through to make most
chowders, however complicated, worth eating.

Chowders differ from locale to locale, from state to state.
Some use milk; some have no milk. One chowder bearing the
name of a state utilizes tomato soup. Most chowders have this
much in common: they contain clams and, usually, some portion
of the liquid from the clams. I sometimes commit the cardinal
sin—in the eyes of dyed-in-the-wool clam lovers—and discard
the liquor of the clams entirely, for the clam itself is strong

enough to impart the flavor to a chowder. I have also been known to make a chowder of unchopped or unground small, tender clams.

The basic Southern Chowder is the one I usually make; and I vary it to suit my mood, sometimes even putting in a couple of diced carrots. You'll note that the recipe calls for frying some grease out of fatback for seasoning, but this step may be considered optional. Also, the thickening agent may be left out, reducing the list of ingredients to clams, potatoes, onions, salt, and pepper.

Southern Chowder

2 cups (more or less) ground clams	6 (more or less) medium-sized potatoes, diced
Clam liquor	1 small onion, diced
2 or 3 slices salt pork	Salt and pepper to taste

2 tablespoons cornmeal

Grind or chop clams in liquor. Render fat from salt pork by frying. Put clams and liquor, potatoes, and onions into a saucepan and add water to cover. Season with fat from salt pork and salt and pepper. Cook until potatoes are done. Make gravy of cornmeal and a small amount of water and pour in to give slight body to soup. Cook for fifteen minutes longer.

Long Island Clam Chowder

2 cups ground or chopped clams	3 large tomatoes, peeled and chopped
2 or 3 slices salt pork	1 medium-sized onion, chopped
Clam liquor	
1 cup celery, chopped	½ teaspoon thyme

Salt and pepper to taste

Render fat from pork in pot and remove pork. Add all ingredients, including clam liquor, and dilute with water to cover. Simmer for three hours. Let cool. Chill overnight. When ready to serve, heat chowder, but do not allow it to boil.

New England Clam Chowder

4 cups ground or chopped clams	2 cups water
2 or 3 slices salt pork, diced	2½ cups scalded milk
1 medium-sized onion	½ cup cream
3 cups potatoes, diced	2 tablespoons butter
	Clam liquor

Render out salt pork in pot until almost crisp. Add onions and simmer about five minutes, or until onions are soft. Add potatoes, water, and clam liquor. Cover and simmer about ten minutes. Add clams, scalded milk, and cream. Cook slowly about twenty minutes, or until potatoes are tender. Add butter.

Rhode Island Clam Chowder

In the preceding recipe, use one cup canned tomato soup in place of the cup of milk.

New York Clam Chowder

4 cups ground or chopped clams	1 medium onion, diced
Clam liquor and water to make six cups	½ cup celery, chopped
4 or 5 slices salt pork, diced	1 small garlic clove, chopped
2½ cups potatoes, diced	½ teaspoon thyme
1 cup carrots, diced	1 teaspoon salt
	2 cups canned tomatoes
	1 teaspoon Worcestershire

Black pepper to taste

Fry salt pork in pot until crisp. Add garlic, potatoes, carrots, onions, and celery. Simmer about ten minutes. Add clams, tomatoes, liquor, water, and seasonings. Cook slowly until vegetables are done.

Clam Chowder with Rice

2 *cups ground or chopped*   ½ *teaspoon salt*
   clams   *Black pepper to taste*
2 *or 3 slices salt pork, diced*   ½ *cup rice*
1 *medium onion, diced*   *Clam liquor*

Render fat from salt pork in cooking vessel. Add onions and cook until tender. Add clams, rice, salt, pepper, and clam liquor with enough water to make three cups of liquid. Cook until rice is done. Thickness of chowder may be varied by altering the amount of rice and water used. As with most chowders, reheating adds to the flavor.

When Roasted Crabs
Hiss in the Bowl

THESE ARE DARK DAYS FOR CRABS. IN 1968 SOME PACKERS OF CRAB-
meat reported that their catch was down as much as 75%. All
along the Eastern Seaboard the summer of '68 was spent in

search of the blue crabs which had always been so plentiful.*

In Maryland, crabbers blamed the shortage on Virginia watermen, who, they said, dredged female crabs out of the lower Chesapeake Bay during the egg-laying period. Others around the Chesapeake blamed the heavy spring rains which diluted the salt content of the Upper Bay. However, the shortage of crabs along the famous Chesapeake was not an isolated phenomenon. Crab men from Maryland to Florida reported that there were just no crabs. In my own back yard, attempts to take crabs from the saltwater creek beside the marsh were useless until late summer. Local crab processors had to buy crabs from other localities. Late in the year, a newspaper story announced the establishment of a survey to determine why blue crabs were dying by the thousands.

Before this year it was so easy to catch crabs that the temptation was to take too many, as we did the first time we decided to have a crab feast. We were living in Fayetteville and spent most weekends driving to one of the beaches. We would alternate between Emerald Isle and Holden's Beach, favoring them because both offered long stretches of dunes where one could find some privacy. We were on a shell-collecting kick and would spend days walking the beach, digging in odoriferous mud flats, and snorkeling in the shallow parts of the inlets. We found wentletraps and angel wings and a couple of weathered Scotch bonnets, but we usually ate hamburgers because cooking would have taken time away from our shell-hunting.

---

*Nineteen sixty-nine, on the other hand, was a banner year for crabs, with supply so plentiful that prices paid to crab gatherers dropped as low as four cents per pound. However, there are still dark clouds on the horizon, with North Carolina scientists involved in a search for the cause of a new crab-killing disease which broke out during the summer.

The day we went crab fishing, we had organized a party to visit Holden's Beach. There were a couple who lived across the street from us, a friend from my home town who was stationed at Fort Bragg, my young daughter, my wife, and I. Our friends balked at wading a muddy marsh looking for shells, and someone suggested that we go fishing. We had no tackle, of course, so we settled for the next best thing—fishing for crabs from a shrimp-house dock. We bought a piece of fatback from a little store, dug a few lengths of old fishing line out of the back of the car, and began to catch blue crabs by the dozen. We didn't even have a net. The crabs were so eager to be caught that they'd hang onto the fatback all the way up through the air to the dock and into an old basket someone had found somewhere. Enthusiasm ran high. We were going to go back to Fayetteville and have one grand crab feast.

A bushel basket full of crabs is a lot of crabs, and a sunny, long, full day of beaching is pleasantly tiring. We drove home with a trunk full of crabs but lost all of our support immediately. Our bachelor friend faded away while we weren't looking, saying he had early reveille. The couple from across the street said they definitely wanted to eat some crabs and would be back to help clean them as soon as they could take a quick shower. That was at nine o'clock. At ten, we decided our friends had finked out for good; and there, outside the door, was a bushel basket full of squirming crabs.

"Let us begin," my wife said, and we did. We dropped some of the protesting crabs into hot water, boiled them pink, and began to pick out the meat. We were determined not to waste a single crab. We would carry on, regardless of the pleasant tiredness which had now become bone weariness. We would pick every crab, freeze the meat, and have crab for months whenever we wanted it.

There were some things, however, that we had not considered. I took my first taste of crab meat—a white morsel from the boiled body of a crab from which I'd just washed the unappetiz-ing-looking gills. Gaaaa. "Well," I said, "maybe you have to acquire a taste for crab meat."

We picked. We threw more of those poor little beasts into boiling water, and that cruelty alone almost turned my stomach. The kitchen reeked. Bits of crab meat and waste were spread everywhere. And I had my bedamned code. Don't kill it unless you're going to eat it or use it. My wife, game to the end, held out longer than I did. With only one-third of the basket of crabs processed, I gave up. I had a sunburn. I was nauseous. I was tired. It was two o'clock in the morning.

Next day, when the garbage men lifted my garbage can, they heard little scraping sounds from inside. When they opened the lid, out jumped an angry blue crab. When they poured the con-tents of the garbage can into the truck, blue crabs scuttled every-where.

Well, what else are you going to do with live crabs a hundred miles from salt water?

I knew a man in Fayetteville who solved the same problem, an oversupply of crabs, by dumping them on the front porch of a friend; but I'm not a practical joker.

Neither my wife nor I ever ate one puny bite of the ap-proximately one-half pint of crab meat that we picked that night. For years I wouldn't even eat the crab cake on a seafood platter. I never really learned to appreciate the blue crab as a food until I made the acquaintance of a can of prepared claw fingers from Cash Caroon's processing plant. My Elizabeth, who had cheated and eaten crab meat now and again after our traumatic experience with live crabs, brought home a can of the claw fingers; and, since they had already been paid for and I hate waste, I tried them.

Crab meat picked and prepared by someone else is fitten'!

Heck, crab meat picked by yourself is fine, after you learn the tricks of the trade. I think a lot of people don't like crab meat because they were introduced to it the way I was. Dumping a crab, alive, into boiling water is no fit preparation for a pleasant meal. Cleaning a crab after he's cooked, then eating him after scraping out the wastes and the—ugh—"devil's fingers" and stuff like that, takes a stronger stomach than mine. To me, crab meat has a rich, heavy taste—a taste that can easily be spoiled by unappetizing sights and smells.

+ My smart wife, who found that she rather liked crab meat and definitely enjoyed catching crabs, has devised a means of preparing them that does not offend my delicate tummy. Instead of dumping them into boiling water and watching them kick, she kills them mercifully with an icepick. Instead of cooking them whole and then trying to clean them, she cleans them first and then cooks what is left—the edible meat in the shelly body cavities and in the claws. A cleaned crab body, cooked, is white and clean-looking. The taste, to me, is delicate and delicious when the waste parts are removed before cooking. I now like crab meat.

Some crab eaters say that there is no flavor to a crab that has been cleaned before cooking, and some swear by the taste added by the accumulated fat of a crab—fat which we carefully clean away. Some even cook a female with her eggs and say that this enhances the flavor. I'll be completely open-minded. Those who favor such practices are perfectly free to write their own cookbooks and pass along their barbaric beliefs.

CLEANING CRABS

Actually, there are two ways of cleaning a crab—the professional way and my way. Then, too, there is a difference in the way crabs are picked in a large processing house and the way they are picked at home. There's also a difference in the way crabs are cooked. In a processing house, the crabs are cooked for about twenty minutes under pressure. The steam and the high temperature sterilize the crab and, judging from looks only, cook the crab more thoroughly. It's possible that the professional crab pickers just make it look easier, but it seems to me that a crab cooked by the commercial process is easier to pick than a boiled crab.

Crab plants separate the meat into different types to go into different products. Ordinarily, the home cook need not worry too much about separating the meat when it's picked from the crab.

Pro crab pickers use a small knife about the size of a kitchen paring knife but with a smaller blade that is thin from back to front so that it will go down into the cavities in a crab's body and claws. Since the workers are paid by the amount of production, they are fast; and they have a particular way to do every little movement.

First, the large claws are pulled from the crab with a twisting motion. The knife is inserted at the front of the shell, and the top of the shell is pulled off in one easy motion, leaving the crab body bared. The legs are then cut away from the body, with the cutting being done close to the body. With the sharp side of the knife blade, two quick slices remove the gills. The white meat is plucked out of the body cavities with the tip of the knife blade, and the white meat clinging to the bottom of the removed gills is picked away.

In picking the claws, the sharp side of the knife is used to crack-cut the shell of the upper joint at about the midpoint. The shell is struck as if one were cracking an egg shell with a knife, so that the knife does not cut into the meat. The upper joint is then broken open at the cut-break with the fingers, and the meat is plucked out of the upper joint with the point of the knife.

A sharp, egg-shell-cracking blow with the knife blade just above the claw fingers allows the shell to be broken with one's fingers. If the cracking has been done just right, and if the tide and the moon and the astrological signs are just right, the meat clings in a juicy morsel to the thin cartilage extending from the claw fingers. If this happens—and even the pros miss a good percentage of the time—the movable claw finger is broken away, leaving the fixed finger as an eating handle. If the meat pulls away from the claw finger and remains in the round cavity of the shell, it is picked out with the point of the knife blade.

Prepared claw fingers, a specialty item available here and there where there is a crab-processing plant around, are, to my taste, the choicest part of the crab. One plant owner said that he was able to develop only two expert claw-finger-makers out of a hundred pickers. One eats claw fingers by picking them up by the base of the claw and pulling the very tasty meat away from the cartilage with the teeth in one easy motion. They're great for party snacks, dipped in a sauce of one's choice.

When a crab is cooked whole under pressure with steam, it is slightly dried out. The gills, or "devil's fingers," are a neat, greyish mass which can be cut away easily. Boiling a crab—

the usual home-cooking method—adds water to the meat, making the inside of the crab more mushy and more messy.

My semipro crab-picker has developed a way to beat the smell and the mess. Her equipment includes an icepick, a forceps-type gadget left over from our last baby—it was used to pluck baby bottles out of boiling water—an old pair of scissors, and a sharp knife.

The forceps are used to hold the crab. It's possible to hold a crab with your bare hands if you seize him firmly from the rear so that he can't get to you with his claws. However, if you have a mess of crabs, they're probably all entangled in a basket or some other container. The forceps enable you to reach into the squirming pile of ill temper and bring out a single crab.

An icepick pushed through the crab just behind the eyes is a quick and merciful means of slaughter.

When the crab's claws go limp and he ceases to fight, break the large claws off at the body and put them aside.

Seize the crab firmly in one hand; with the other hand, lift the apron on the bottom of the crab's shell. It may be necessary to insert a knife blade under the tip of the apron to lift it. Pull it all the way back, ripping it away from the body.

Turn the crab over and put steady pressure on the top part of the shell until it tears away from the body. Large shells may be cleaned and saved for use in cooking baked or deviled crabs.

With an old pair of scissors or a sharp knife, cut the flipper-legs away from the crab's body at the last joint next to the body.

The exposed innards of the crab will show stomach and entrails at the front in a little cavity between two peaked, compartmented, cartilage-covered areas of white meat. Atop the peaked areas will be perched the gills—soft, spongy masses that can be removed by scraping or pulling away from the body.

A portion of the stomach may be pulled out along with the top shell. After cleaning the remainder of the soft mass away from the cavity, wash the crab thoroughly.

The white, edible meat is left inside the little compartments, the whole contained in the bottom shell and the interior cartilage. The crab body is now ready for boiling or frying.

BUYING CRABS AND CRAB MEAT

Whole crabs, either hard- or soft-shelled, should be kicking when purchased, and not just moving a feeble flipper now and then, either. A hard-shell blue crab is a cantankerous individual. When he's fit to eat, he's mad—spitting at you and ready to chew you a little with his claw.

Crabs keep for a while out of water. My neighbor brought home a mess of crabs one night and put them in a covered basket outside his door. During the night a prowling coon or fox or dog overturned the basket, and next morning the lawn was covered with angry blue crabs. One, leaping out from the shelter of a gardenia bush, attacked a neighborhood child, leaving a red welt on her ankle.

By far the most labor-free way of getting crab meat is to buy it already processed. With variations from locale to locale, processed crab meat may be purchased fresh, pasteurized, frozen, or canned. I don't want to hurt the feelings of anyone, so I'll point out that the following is a direct quote from our local crab expert. I wouldn't have the courage to fly into the teeth of vested interests with such a statement, but our crab expert is a brave man, as witness the fact that he is running for the Board of County Commissioners on the Republican ticket.

Sez he, "Fresh crab meat is a little better than pasteurized crab meat, and pasteurized crab meat is a little better than

frozen crab meat, and canned crab meat is only a substitute."
So there.

Fresh crab meat will keep two or three days under ordinary
refrigeration. It will keep for a week if it is iced and then refrig-
erated. Crab meat, picked out, freezes well. As soon after picking as possible, freeze in its own juice in an airtight container.

Never freeze whole crabs. They dehydrate to nothing in no
time at all.

The taste of crab meat is often described as "sweet." I dunno.
I think "ripe" when I think of the taste of crab meat.

Whatever the descriptive term used and whether you choose
to clean a crab my way or some other way, the taking and selling
of blue crabs is a big business. And crabbing for pleasure and
for one's own dinner continues to be one of the more pleasant
ways of spending an afternoon. A commercial crabber running
a hundred crab pots and working hard at it can make a couple
of hundred bucks a week during the seasons, which are loosely
spring and fall. Live crabs sold to processors for an average of
ten cents a pound in 1967, and some North Carolina processors
had to import crabs from Virginia because the local supply was
not enough to meet the demand. Processors like the Caroon
Crab Company of Southport have trouble keeping up with the
demand for picked crab meat, and you have to be there at the
right time to be able to buy a can of claw fingers.

The crab industry has seen a spectacular growth. North Carolina crabbers currently take about twenty-five million pounds
a year, as compared to about five and a half million pounds in
1945, for example.

HOW AND WHEN TO TAKE CRABS

There aren't any crabs in winter. You can fish for them all

day, and they don't come to the bait. That's because they go dormant and burrow into the bottom mud when the temperature of the water falls below the low fifties. In the spring, when things warm up, the crabs begin to crawl.

You can find crabs almost anywhere in saltwater creeks, rivers, sounds, and inlets. Fishermen find them too often, for crabs are champion bait stealers. A place where there is an artificial supply of food, such as near a shrimp house where the shrimp heads are dumped into the water, makes an excellent crabbing spot. Crabs don't store the nasty little bugs that oysters and other shellfish pick up from dirty water, so even Cape Fear crabs are O.K. to eat.

The way to get crabs that is the most fun is with a hand line and a chunk of meat. No hook is needed on the line, since the crab clings to the bait with his claws and is dipped up with a net. There's a cheap, long-handled dip net on the market that is designed especially for crabbing. The bait can be anything from leftover steak to a fish head; but tough salt pork is also good because it will stay on the line for a long time and become seasoned over a period of days to a ripeness that cannot be resisted by any crab within a hundred yards. Let the bait sink to the bottom. It may be necessary to weight the meat to get it to stay down. When something tries to walk off with it, pull in slowly and evenly until you have raised the bait and the feeding crab to the surface of the water. Dip the net under Mr. Crab and repeat.

For real gone crab lovers who don't want to waste time catching them by hand, a crab pot is a good investment. Actually, a crab pot in this part of the country is nothing more than a wire trap of the same type as that used to catch blackfish. It's called a pot, I suppose, because lobster pots are called pots or because the term is simply one of those long-accepted salticisms that makes the user of the term feel nautical. The pot is baited with some animal tissue and submerged in salt water; and, presto, crabs enter and cannot escape.

The pots should be worked now and then. Crabs chew on each other if confined in small spaces and even die occasionally. Pro crab trappers work their traps every day.

One sad offshoot of trapping came to my attention one day at the Long Beach Marina. We checked two long-neglected crab pots suspended below a bridge and found a lovely, but thoroughly dead, otter in each trap. Since otters, next to girls, are my favorite animals, I was saddened. Probably, however, the miniature double tragedy would have happened even if the crabber had checked his pots daily; for the otter is, of course, an air-breathing mammal and couldn't have survived long after being trapped in the crab pot.

Crabbers used to use a baited trotline to catch crabs. Perhaps they still do. In big, sheltered waters, such as the northern North Carolina sounds and Chesapeake Bay, a thousand feet of trotline was not unusual. The trotline is worked as long as it's in the water, the bait being something cheap and plentiful, such as eel. Automated trotlines, with rollers and dip bags so that the line is worked merely by putting it over a roller and moving the boat forward, may use as much as a mile of line.

But for the casual crabber, hand-line fishing is pleasant and rewarding and is also an excellent way to entertain young children for an afternoon.

COOKING A CRAB

Aside from frying the entire crab body, the standard way to cook a crab is to drop him into boiling water. Even if the meat is to be baked or prepared in some other way later, boiling comes first. If the crabs are to be eaten in a cocktail or just as boiled crabs, commercially prepared crab boils are popular. They contain spices such as sage and nutmeg, and the main purpose, or at least the main result, of their use is to lessen the rather crabby smell of boiling crabs. The meat is encased in shell or cartilage and is not much affected by the seasonings.

How long should crabs be boiled? Until the claws turn a bright pink. The cleaned crab bodies will not show this change in color to the same extent as the claws, so gauge the cooking time by the larger claws. A couple of minutes more after they turn pink won't hurt anything, either. However, as with most seafoods, it's very easy to overcook.

Now comes the fun part. After letting the crabs cool, it's necessary to pick them if you want crab meat for cocktails or other use. For a meal of boiled crabs, I highly suggest the community pick-out type of meal. Just serve the boiled bodies and claws with a sauce and crackers and a sharp knife and, perhaps, some nutcrackers. Eating crabs this way is not neat, so forget about having a nice-looking table and provide newspapers or layers of paper towels to keep the crab fluids from running all over the table; and be sure to have containers into which to dump the shells and cartilage.

Picking a boiled, cleaned crab is not too difficult. Use a sharp knife to cut away the lower shell and then use the tip of the knife, a nutpick, or a small olive fork to pick the meat out of the small cavities. The claws may be attacked in two ways. Either use a nutcracker or, if you're eating outside or cleaning them on a cutting board, whack them with the blade of a knife to crack-cut the shell. Then break the shell open with your fingers and pick out the meat.

Crab Cocktail

   Providing a bowl of boiled crab, to be picked and eaten, with a sauce and a cracker or two, is the most basic way of serving crab. The crab cocktail is a minor variation in which the hostess, or someone, does all the work. After the crabs are picked, the meat is arranged on a lettuce leaf or in a glass container and served with a sauce of your choice.

Fried Crab

Crab bodies	*Egg*
Mealing mixture	*Milk*
	Salt and pepper

Salt and pepper crab bodies, dip in milk-egg mixture, and roll in mealing mixture. Fry in deep fat at 375° about five minutes, or until brown; or fry in shallow fat until brown.

Baked Crab

1

1 *pound crab meat*	*Dash Worcestershire*
¼ *cup mayonnaise*	*Tabasco to taste*
1 *teaspoon pimiento, chopped*	1 *teaspoon salt*
	Paprika

Mix all ingredients except crab and paprika. Pour mixture over crab meat and stir lightly. Bake in crab shells or in shallow baking dish at 350° about twenty-five minutes, or until well browned. Sprinkle with paprika.

2

1 *pound crab meat*	*Salt to taste*
¼ *cup lemon juice*	*Pepper to taste*
½ *cup melted butter*	*Paprika*

Pour butter and lemon juice over crab meat and mix lightly. Salt and pepper. Bake at 450° for ten to fifteen minutes, or until well browned. Sprinkle with paprika.

Steamed Crab

1 *pound crab meat*	1 *tablespoon vinegar*
3 *tablespoons water*	1 *tablespoon butter*

Salt and pepper to taste

Bring water and vinegar to a boil. Add crab meat and cover. Simmer for five minutes. Add butter and heat until butter blends. Salt and pepper. Serve either hot or cold with crackers.

Barbecued Crab

3 *cups crab meat*	1 *cup tomato juice*
1 *cup celery, chopped*	2 *tablespoons Worcestershire*
1 *onion, chopped*	3 *or 4 peppercorns*
1 *garlic clove, chopped*	*Bit of crushed bay leaf*
¼ *cup salad oil*	½ *cup soy sauce*
2 *cups bouillon*	*Dash or two of Tabasco*

Cook celery, onions, and garlic in oil until tender. Add bouillon, tomato juice, Worcestershire, peppercorns, and bay leaf. Cook on low heat, covered, about thirty or forty minutes. Add soy sauce and Tabasco and strain through colander. Add crab meat to strained liquid and simmer for twenty minutes.

Charcoaled Soft-Shells

1 *dozen soft-shell crabs*   ¼ *teaspoon nutmeg*
¼ *teaspoon soy sauce*   1 *teaspoon lemon juice*
¾ *cup parsley, chopped*   ½ *cup cooking oil*
                    Dash Tabasco

Make sauce of all ingredients except crabs. Cook crabs over charcoal, either in hinged wire grill or directly on grill, basting liberally with sauce. Cook about eight or ten minutes per side.

Crab Casserole

1

2 *cups cooked crab meat*   2 *teaspoons Worcestershire*
2 *cans mushroom soup*   ½ *teaspoon salt*
2 *boiled eggs, diced*   *Pepper to taste*
2 *teaspoons lemon juice*   2 *teaspoons melted butter*
                ¼ *cup bread crumbs*

Mix all ingredients except butter and bread crumbs. Put in baking dish and top with butter and crumbs. Bake at 400° about twenty minutes.

2

1 *pound crab meat*   6 *boiled eggs, chopped*
4 *tablespoons butter*   2 *green peppers, chopped*
4 *tablespoons flour*   1 *tablespoon prepared mustard*
1 *teaspoon salt*   2 *tablespoons mayonnaise*
Black pepper to taste   *Dash of nutmeg*
2 *cups milk*   2 *tablespoons lemon juice*
                Mild, yellow cheese, grated

Make a white sauce by melting butter in saucepan and blending in flour, salt, and pepper. Remove from heat and stir in milk. Cook, stirring constantly, until smooth. Set aside to cool. Mix crab meat and other ingredients, except cheese, and place in crab shells or baking dish. Top with cheese and bake at about 400° for fifteen minutes. Pour white sauce over and reheat. Serve hot.

Deviled Crab

1

1 *pound crab meat*	1 *teaspoon prepared mustard*
2 *eggs, beaten*	*Tabasco to taste*
1 *green pepper, chopped*	1 *cup evaporated milk*
1 *small onion, chopped*	*Salt and pepper*
Salad oil	*Cleaned crab shells*
2 *tablespoons mayonnaise*	*Paprika*

Cook green pepper and onions in small amount of oil until tender. Mix with other ingredients, except paprika, and put into crab shells. Sprinkle with paprika. Bake at 350° for twenty minutes, or until golden brown.

2

2 *cups crab meat*	½ *teaspoon dry mustard*
2 *cups milk*	*Dash cayenne pepper*
5 *boiled eggs, separated*	½ *cup melted butter*
1½ *teaspoons salt*	1½ *cups bread crumbs*

Combine milk, crab meat, and chopped whites of eggs. Blend in mashed yolks of eggs. Add salt, mustard, and cayenne pepper. Sprinkle with buttered crumbs and bake in crab shells or in casserole dish at 450° for fifteen minutes, or until golden brown.

Crab Cake

1 *pound crab meat*   1 *teaspoon prepared mustard*
½ *cup bread crumbs*   ¼ *teaspoon Worcestershire*
1 *egg, beaten*   ½ *teaspoon salt*
1 *tablespoon mayonnaise*   *Pepper to taste*

Combine ingredients and form into patties. Fry in small amount of cooking oil until golden brown. Makes ten or twelve patties.

Tossed Crab Salad

½ *pound crab meat*   *Small head lettuce, chopped*
½ *cup salad oil*   1 *cup celery, diced*
¼ *cup salad vinegar*   1 *cup olives, sliced*
                    Salt and pepper

Mix salad oil and vinegar and pour over crab meat in shallow dish. Let stand for thirty minutes in cool place. Drain. Toss lightly with lettuce, celery, and olives. Serve with salad dressing, salt, and pepper.

Caroon's Crab Salad

1 *pound crab meat*   2 *tablespoons mayonnaise*
¼ *cup celery, diced*   2 *tbsp. sweet pickle vinegar*
3 *hard-boiled eggs, diced*   1 *teaspoon Worcestershire*
¼ *cup sweet pickles, diced*   *Salt and pepper to taste*
                    Paprika

Mix ingredients gently and serve on lettuce boats with sprigs of parsley. Sprinkle with paprika.

Crabmeat with Rice

1 *pound cooked crab meat*	2 *cups canned tomatoes*
4 *slices bacon, chopped*	¼ *cup uncooked rice*
½ *cup onions, chopped*	1 *teaspoon Worcestershire*
½ *cup celery, chopped*	½ *teaspoon salt*
½ *cup green pepper, chopped*	*Pepper to taste*

Render fat from bacon. Add onions, celery, and green pepper and cook until tender. Add tomatoes, rice, and seasonings. Simmer, covered, for twenty minutes, or until rice is done. Add crab meat and reheat.

NOTE: The above recipe is greatly enhanced for lovers of hot stuff by the addition of two or three very hot little peppers, fresh, if they are in season.

Crab Stuffing

1 *pound crab meat*	⅓ *cup cooking oil*
½ *cup onion, chopped*	2 *cups bread cubes*
⅓ *cup celery, chopped*	3 *eggs, beaten*
⅓ *cup green pepper, chopped*	1 *tablespoon parsley, chopped*
	2 *teaspoons salt*
1 *clove garlic, chopped*	*Pepper to taste*

Drain crab meat. Cook onions, celery, green pepper, and garlic in cooking oil until tender. Combine with other ingredients and mix. Use for stuffing fish, shrimp, or other seafood.

Crabcumbers

2 *cups crab meat*	3-*ounce package cream cheese*
6 *medium cucumbers*	1 *tbsp. horseradish (optional)*
1 *can whole pimientos*	1 *tablespoon lemon juice*

Scoop out inside of cucumbers with small knife. Mix other ingredients, stuff inside cucumbers, and chill. Serve with crackers.

Chili Crab in Green Peppers

1 *pound crab meat*	2 *tablespoons lemon juice*
6 *green peppers*	¼ *teaspoon Worcestershire*
½ *cup mayonnaise*	½ *cup chili sauce*
¼ *cup onion, chopped*	*Tabasco to taste*
2 *boiled eggs, chopped*	1 *teaspoon salt*

1 *cup boiling water*

Boil green peppers for five minutes, after cutting tops away and removing seeds. Mix remaining ingredients, except half of the chili sauce, adding one cup boiling water last. (If crab meat is very moist, use less boiling water.) Stuff green peppers with mixture and bake in greased pan at 425° about twenty-five minutes, or until brown. Heat remaining chili sauce and distribute over top of stuffed peppers.

Stuffed Avocados

1 *pound crab meat*	¼ *teaspoon Worcestershire*
3 *or 4 ripe avocados*	2 *tbsp. pimiento, chopped*
2 *tablespoons butter*	2 *tablespoons olives, chopped*
2 *tablespoons flour*	¼ *teaspoon salt*
1 *cup milk*	*Pepper to taste*

¼ *cup yellow cheese, grated*

Melt butter. Blend in flour. Add milk and cook until thick, stirring constantly. Add seasonings, pimiento, olives, and crab meat. Cut avocados in half and remove seeds. Stuff with crab mixture, sprinkle with cheese, and bake at 350° for twenty to twenty-five minutes, or until brown.

Party Sandwiches

1 *pound cooked crab meat*	2 *tablespoons salad vinegar*
½ *cup almonds, chopped*	*Salt and pepper to taste*
3 *tablespoons mayonnaise*	*Toasted bread*

Mix ingredients and serve on cut squares of toasted bread.

CRABOLOGY

What does a crab have to be so crabby about? How would you like to grow about one-third of your size in a couple of hours? And have to shell out of your skin and walk around in your bones fifteen or so times in your life? And on top of all that, have a life span of only two or three years? Then people want to toss you into boiling water while you're still alive. It's enough to give anyone a bad disposition.

In the beginning, a crab comes from a large family. His ma, who has been seized roughly and impregnated by a rugged male while she is without protection, while she is molting and without a shell, lays a couple of million eggs. These eggs form an orange mass which clings to the lower body of the female crab for about fifteen days. Then each egg becomes a zoea—tiny, unprotected, free-swimming, often eaten by just about anything that's hungry. The zoea molts a few times and becomes a megalops, no larger than before. About a month after the egg is hatched, the megalops looks like a crab, settles to the bottom, and begins gaining weight. When the poor crab gets so cramped in his shell that conditions are no longer tolerable, he cracks his shell, bursts out of it, and is completely defenseless again for a couple of hours until a new shell hardens.

During the few hours of being a soft-shell, the crab is prey for other crabs, birds, fish, and humans. Soft-shells hide in the sand or weeds to save themselves from being eaten; then, once their shells are hard again, they go out and try to eat other soft-shell crabs.

While soft, females get raped by males; but two or so breedings is all a female has to endure before death. In 1737, John Brickell wrote about natural history in North Carolina and innocently assumed that the male crab was protecting the soft-shell crab to which it was attached. It was sorta sweet and naive of the old fellow to assume that the crab became his brother's keeper when all the time that lousy male crab was attached to that poor, soft-shell female for his own vile and carnal satisfaction.

The female crab has her revenge, however, with the help of man. It seems that the male crab is fatter and has more edible meat. You can tell a male from a female by body shape, but this takes more knowledge of crabs than most people want. The easiest way is to look at the crab's belly. There, in the lower abdomen, is a little shell formation called the apron. If I can induce the illustrator to produce some mildly pornographic pictures (at least a crab might think they are suggestive), we will see that the female apron is rounded while the male apron is pointed. Male pointed; female rounded. Get it?

Female Apron   Male Apron

Some people, as I have said, include eggs in their crab meat; others advise tossing back a female with a sponge of orange eggs showing. As far as I've been able to find out, there are no restrictions on the private individual who takes crabs for his own use; so let your conscience be your guide, I suppose. I, personally, will toss back a spawning female and get a couple of those horny old male crabs who attack those defenseless females and who have more meat to them anyhow.

Most soft-shell crabs are not caught. That is, they're not caught while they're soft-shelled. People who produce soft-shelled crabs for the market have large tanks in which they incarcerate green crabs. Green crabs are those who are happy, for the moment, in their hard shells. When the green crab becomes a peeler, that is, when he begins to show signs of shedding his temporary overcoat, he is transferred to the peeler tank. Sometimes the crab is inflicted with the indignity of having his claws broken so that he will not do bodily damage to other peelers. When the peeler bursts out of his body, he is known as a buster and is put into another tank to allow him to complete the process of molting. Then, during the short period during which he is soft—wham! chow time. As far as I can find out, soft-shell crab operations are mainly in the northern part of the state.

If you catch a crab, pick him, and find that he has very little meat, he's probably a buckram, a newly molted crab. Shedding one's outer bones is strenuous work, and growing one-third of one's original size within hours also tends to cut down the flesh on one's bones. This growth thing is fantastic. It's almost a Ripley type experience to see the old shell and the new crab side by side.

When a crab reaches adulthood, after about the fifteenth shedding of his shell, he ceases to grow. Oh, he'll gain weight in the shell, but he's as big as he's going to get on the outside. Now and then you'll run across an old granddaddy, who may be all of three years old, with oysters and barnacles on his shell. He's past the breeding stage and is waiting only for his old-age pension, so you may as well eat him.

It is true that a crab can regrow a claw. However, there are limitations to the marvelous ability to do so. A crab can drop a claw if he needs to take it on the lam, and then he can regrow it. If the claw is parted from his body without mangling violence, he can regrow the claw; but if it is wrested away and the surrounding tissues are torn and ruptured, it's good-bye claw.

Shrympes and a Litull Salt

THE SHRIMP IS A CRUSTACEAN, A RELATIVE OF CRABS, LOBSTERS, barnacles, sand fleas, and wood lice. Like the crab, the shrimp wears his bones on the outside and has to shed the whole bit when he wants to grow. Fortunately, the shrimp seems to grow as well as he does anything, shooting up to as much as six inches in length in a year.

Prawns, which are not shrimp but are of the same immediate family, only larger, grow even more spectacularly than shrimp. In western Australia's Shark Bay, tiger prawns up to ten inches long are caught for the export market.

In this country, the little shrimp is the foundation for a one-hundred-million-dollar industry. United States shrimp boats landed 312.2 million pounds of shrimp in 1967, making this country the shrimp-eating champion of the world, followed by India, Japan, Mexico, Brazil, Thailand, West Germany, Pakistan, and the Netherlands. And in addition to the shrimp we catch, we import shrimp from Mexico, Panama, India, Guyana, and Pakistan.

When the first interstate shipments of shrimp were made, back in 1910 or 1912, shrimpers in Fernandina Beach, Florida, boiled shrimp, salted them in layers in a barrel, and sent them off via Railway Express to New York. New York continued to be the chief market for shrimp for many years. It was not until after World War II that shrimp began to appear widely on inland menus.

Now, shrimp is probably the number one favorite of the nation in the way of seafoods. Because shrimp can be frozen so successfully, either untreated or breaded, they're available to cooks in the middle of the Great American Desert. People who come to the coast for the first time, people who have not had the opportunity of making the acquaintance of, say, a fresh oyster, already know and like shrimp.

Shipyards from North Carolina to Texas are turning out shrimp boats just about as fast as they can be built, until it would seem that the little shrimp could not possibly support any more fishing. Yet it does. One reason for the continued expansion of the shrimp-fishing industry is the discovery of new shrimping grounds. Huge seagoing shrimpers travel from hot spot to hot spot, trying to beat the other fellows to the big pickings, getting into minor wars now and then with the authorities of Latin countries bordering the Gulf of Mexico.

From time to time, new species of shrimp are discovered in commercial quantities. At the moment, the excitement in the shrimping industry comes largely from a species called Royal-Red. Unlike the usual run of shrimp, the Royal-Red likes deep water. One large Royal-Red ground is off the east coast of Florida at 140 to 260 fathoms. Translated from salty talk, those shrimp are darned deep—840 to 1,560 feet down. Other Royal-Red grounds have been found around the Dry Tortugas, southwest of the Florida peninsula, and off the coasts of Louisiana, Mississippi, and Alabama in the Gulf.

Rich shrimping grounds have also been found in the past few years off the northeastern shoulder of South America, with bases in Guyana, Surinam, French Guiana, and the islands of Barbados and Trinidad.

Meantime, back on the North Carolina coast, creeks, marshes, and rivers continue to be spawning grounds for edible shrimp which, though not as spectacular as the Royal-Reds and Australia's tiger prawns, make some fine eating.

The shrimp docks are colorful and as salty as the Ancient Mariner himself. There's a smell of fish and of the creosote mixture used to treat the big shrimp nets. The shrimpers have a faraway look in their eyes although they may never get out of sight of land, since most North Carolina shrimping is done close in.

Those who have been in the business for a long time say there are just as many shrimp now as there were twenty years ago, thus disputing the often-heard complaint that the North Carolina area has been shrimped out. Shrimpers say that there are more boats now but that they are landing the same amount of shrimp that used to be landed by far fewer boats. However, one can take shrimp-landing figures for the state and raise a question as to whether or not we're holding our own in shrimp conservation. For example, ten and a half million pounds of shrimp were landed in 1945. In the 1950's, the figures fluctuated wildly from a high of almost eight million pounds in 1957 down to less than half that amount in 1958, and then up to five and a half million pounds in 1966.

Figures for shrimp landings do not include shrimp taken for private use by the many fishermen who have small trawls for outboard boats and who take five or ten pounds of shrimp every time they get hungry for them during the season. Nor do the figures include the amount of shrimp taken by the writer and a certain antique gentleman during two eventful shrimping trips on the Cape Fear and Elizabeth rivers. The first time we went puttin' around, dragging a frail trawl net behind us, picking up a few pounds of hog chokers (small flatfish which look much like baby flounders) and trash and about two quarts of shrimp. My job was to help haul in the net, pick it, and head the shrimp.

Heading a shrimp is a simple matter, except for the horn behind the shrimp's head, which sticks something fierce when you grab it wrong. There are special shrimp-heading knives; and, frankly, I don't know whether the pros use a knife or their thumbnail. People I've seen—mostly part-time shrimpers and me—use their thumbnail, heading shrimp with both hands by pushing the thumbnail behind the shrimp's head and flipping it off.

Our second shrimping trip was a disaster. We pulled the trawl through the old Elizabeth River and were quite elated to feel it getting it heavier and heavier. We were sure we were going to make up for the poor showing of the first trip with a few hundred pounds of nice shrimp. Then we wrapped the net around a piling and tore it loose. After going back to the dock to get a long grappling pole to pull the net up, we found a dozen very large shrimp in the very bottom of the pocket. Talk about the one that got away—I'll bet almost anything that we had thirty pounds of big shrimp—heck, maybe even a hundred pounds—in that net before we wrapped it around the piling.

Small boat shrimping is not a tremendously complicated effort, requiring only a small net equipped with the proper doors, a boat, a motor to pull it, and time. To shrimp the creeks and rivers requires deep water, so shrimping is limited to high-tide time, and high-tide time moves around so that the would-be shrimper must be available at odd hours such as five o'clock in the morning. The big trawlers fish offshore and work at any time they can find shrimp.

There are three main types of shrimp taken by shrimpers in North Carolina waters: the brown spotted shrimp, the brown shrimp, and the white shrimp. The brown spotted shrimp, scarcest of the three, shows first in the spring, reaching commercial size sometime in March. In some years there are not enough of the brown spotted shrimp to make fishing for it commercially feasible. The brown shrimp reaches fishing size sometime between mid-June and the early part of July, and the white shrimp comes along in September.

Shrimpers tell me that North Carolina has one of the better shrimp-conservation programs. Seasons vary slightly. The season will be closed, for example, when fishers begin to catch small white shrimp while taking brown shrimp and will remain closed until the white shrimp are of commercial size.

Shrimp begin to hit the market in the spring and are usually available through Thanksgiving and, sometimes, until Christmas. Shrimp can usually be purchased, either retail or wholesale, at shrimp houses where the fleet docks. Wholesale quantities are lots of twenty-five pounds or more. Shrimp can be purchased either with the heads on or headed. Prices sometimes are almost 50% lower on shrimp with the heads on. Since ten pounds of heads-on shrimp will produce about six pounds of headed shrimp, heads-on shrimp at half the price of headed shrimp is a good buy if you don't mind investing a bit of labor in the heading. Heading is not, as I have indicated, a tough job. Shrimp freeze well, so twenty-five pounds of shrimp is not a tremendous quantity to buy at one time.

FREEZING SHRIMP

Shrimp are headed by separating the head from the body with a shrimp-heading knife or with the thumbnail, but care must be taken not to get stabbed by the pointed horn of the shrimp. Shrimp should be washed thoroughly, using two pans or two sinks. Lifting the shrimp from one pan or sink into another, filled with water, will leave the grit that has been washed off the shrimp in the empty container.

Then the shrimp are put into a container with water and lots of ice, to be chilled as thoroughly as possible in the ice water. The theory here is that the faster shrimp are frozen, the more they're going to taste like fresh shrimp when thawed and cooked. Chilling in the ice water hastens freezing.

The chilled shrimp are then put into freezing containers. Milk cartons are fine, but any container that is watertight may be used. No water is added to the shrimp at this time. The cartons are closed and put into the freezer, with plenty of air space all around the containers so that they are not touching each other or the sides of the freezer. After freezing for twenty-four to forty-eight hours, the containers are removed from the freezer, ice water is poured over the frozen shrimp, and the containers are closed tightly and returned to the freezer.

When shrimp are frozen according to the foregoing method, shrimp-lovers say it's hard to tell frozen shrimp from fresh.

SHELLING AND DEVEINING SHRIMP

East Coast shrimp, while generally smaller than Gulf shrimp, Royal-Reds, or South American shrimp, have some important things going for them as far as we seafood-eaters along the mid-Atlantic Coast are concerned. They're available fresh and fairly economically. Many East Coast shrimp are taken on sandy bottoms, in contrast to the muddy bottom of the Gulf. Shrimp from a sandy bottom, in general, tend to be less gritty than those from a muddy bottom. Small East Coast shrimp usually don't have to be deveined at all.

The hard outer shell of the shrimp is removed as if one were shelling a peanut. Shrimp are shelled for frying and for use in specialty dishes but are boiled with the shells on. Boiled shrimp may be served in the shell, with each person doing his own shelling, or may be shelled before serving. For deep frying, the tail is sometimes left on the shrimp when it is shelled.

If the vein of dark material down the back of a shrimp is quite visible, it is a good idea to remove it, since it can make the shrimp quite gritty. The operation may be done with a sharp knife or with a special deveining tool which is sold in hardware and other stores along the coast. However, if the shrimp is small to medium size and the vein is not prominent, forget it. Deveining is a long, tedious process.

COOKING SHRIMP

There are two basic ways of cooking shrimp: boiling and frying. I've eaten fresh shrimp boiled in nothing but water. Next up the scale of complexity is salted water. In boiling shrimp, the rule for salting is to put in as much salt as you think necessary and then double it. A couple of tablespoons to a large pot of water is not too much if you're boiling shrimp in the shell, the usual way.

The size of the shrimp determines the length of boiling time. Five to ten minutes may be long enough for small shrimp, fifteen minutes for medium. Overcooking makes the shrimp tough and dry. A happy medium is struck when the shrimp are pink and tender.

Some people let boiled shrimp cool a bit in the salted water in which they have been cooked. Others take the shrimp out of the water, sprinkle salt on them, and let them stand for a few minutes.

Many things may be added to the water of a shrimp boil. Popular seasonings include bay leaves, peppercorns, onions, celery, sage, lemon juice, and any other spice or seasoning that strikes the fancy. A commercial crab or shrimp boil preparation may be used. Shrimp stand up pretty well under abuse and come out, mainly, tasting like shrimp.

Boiled Shrimp

5 *pounds shrimp*   2 *tablespoons salt*

Boil shrimp in salted water for ten to fifteen minutes, or until they are pink and tender. Remove from water and sprinkle with salt. Serve with a sauce of your choice, letting each person peel his own shrimp. Serves about 6.

NOTE: Sliced lemon, sliced onion, sliced clove garlic, or other seafood seasonings may be added to the water in which the shrimp are boiled.

Butter-Fried Shrimp

Peeled shrimp   *Butter*
                                    Salt and pepper

If shrimp are large, split open down the back, removing vein in the process. If shrimp are small, use whole. Sprinkle with salt and pepper and let stand for thirty minutes. Fry in butter about five minutes per side, or until brown.

Deep-Fried Shrimp

Peeled shrimp, small   *Mealing mixture*
     to medium   *Egg*
Salt and pepper   *Milk*

Salt and pepper shrimp and let them stand for a few minutes. Dip in egg-milk mixture and roll in mealing mixture. Fry at 375° in deep fat until golden brown.

The solid flesh of the shrimp and its fine taste make it a favorite for inclusion in a variety of baked, broiled, stewed, and boiled dishes. I include here some of the more common shrimp dishes found along the Carolina coast.

Shrimp and Peas

1 *cup shrimp, boiled*   1 *cup milk*
 and peeled   1 *cup tiny English peas,*
2 *tablespoons butter*   *canned or precooked*
2 *tablespoons flour*   *Salt and pepper to taste*

Melt butter. Blend in flour. Add milk and cook until thick, stirring constantly. Add shrimp, peas, salt, and pepper. Reheat.
NOTE: Fine way to use up leftover shrimp from a shrimp boil.

Cantaloupe and Shrimp Cocktail
Shrimp, boiled, peeled, and chilled
Cantaloupe balls or chunks

Serve in chilled glass on lettuce bed with a sauce of your choice.

Closed Top Perloo

1 *pound shrimp, peeled and*   ½ *green pepper, chopped*
 deveined   1 *onion, chopped*
2 *or 3 slices salt pork*   *Salt and pepper*
½ *cup rice*   8-*ounce can tomato sauce*
Stalk celery, chopped   *About 2 cups boiling water*

Render out grease from salt pork in covered pot. Remove pork. Into grease, layer shrimp, rice, chopped ingredients, and more shrimp. Salt and pepper. Pour in tomato sauce. Add boiling water, cover, and simmer for fifteen minutes without opening or stirring. Serve hot.

Boiled Perloo

1 pound shrimp, peeled and
   deveined
2 or 3 slices bacon or fatback
2 cups rice
4 cups water

1 can tomato paste
2 or 3 pieces smoked sausage
   links
1 onion, chopped
Salt and pepper to taste

Render out fatback in iron pot and remove pork from pot. Fry shrimp in grease for three minutes and remove shrimp from pot. Put rice into pot, add water, and cook until half done. Add shrimp, tomato paste, smoked sausage links, onions, bacon, salt, and pepper. Simmer until rice is done.

Shrimp Salad

⅓ lb. shrimp per person
Boiled eggs, chopped
Boiled potato, chopped

Celery, chopped
Sweet pickles, chopped
Mayonnaise
Salt

Boil shrimp, peel, and chop into small pieces. Match the volume of shrimp with eggs and potato, adding celery and pickles to taste. Mix in shrimp. Add enough mayonnaise to smooth the mixture. Salt to taste. Serve on lettuce bed or on toast.

Shrimp Creole

4 lbs. small shrimp, peeled
¾ cup cooking or salad oil
3 tablespoons flour
1 onion, chopped

1 clove garlic, sliced
Salt and pepper to taste
1 large can tomato paste
4 green peppers, chopped

4 cups hot water

Boil shrimp for three minutes. Drain. Mix oil and flour in a pot and brown over low heat. Add onions and garlic and cook until tender. Add shrimp, salt, and pepper. Stir over low heat until gravy covers and coats shrimp, with none sticking to the skillet. Add tomato paste and green peppers. Cook for fifteen minutes over low heat, stirring constantly. Paste must all cling to shrimp with no white showing through. Add one cup hot water, but do not stir. Simmer for fifteen minutes. Stir carefully with fork, being careful not to wash gravy and paste from shrimp. At one side of the pan, gradually add three cups hot water. Simmer for one hour. Serve over rice.

Shrimp Jello

1 cup shrimp, boiled, peeled, and chopped	Dash garlic salt
1 package lemon Jello	Dash black pepper
1 cup hot water	1 tablespoon vinegar
1 teaspoon salt	½ cup cold water
	1 avocado, diced

Dissolve Jello in hot water. Add seasonings and cold water. Pour into a square pan to a depth of about one inch and chill until slightly thickened. Push shrimp and avocado into Jello and chill until firm. Cut into squares to serve.

Potted Shrimp

1 lb. shrimp, boiled and peeled	1 clove garlic, mashed
2 sticks butter	Salt and pepper to taste

Run shrimp through fine food chopper. Cream butter and blend in shrimp, garlic, salt, and pepper. Push through sieve or blend in blender. Serve on fancy crackers or in sandwiches.

Shrimp Casserole

1 *lb. shrimp, boiled and peeled*   1 *can mushroom soup*
1 *large can English peas*   ½ *cup milk*
Salt and pepper

Layer peas and shrimp in greased baking dish. Pour mushroom soup over and add milk. Salt and pepper. Bake at 375° for thirty minutes, or until brown.

I think I'll save my recipes for shrimp and champagne and for dried shrimp until the revised edition comes out. Well, I'll just save the shrimp and champagne. The bit about dried shrimp is too good to keep. It comes from one or the other of the less-developed countries. To dry shrimp, mix brine strong enough to float a potato. Boil headed shrimp in brine for about ten minutes. Put shrimp out on boards in the sun and, after they're pretty well dried, dance on them with wooden shoes to loosen the meat from the hulls.

I like that idea, although I haven't tried it. How about a dried shrimp dancing party, with each guest responsible for bringing his own wooden shoes?

Another recipe I like comes from the fifteenth century English writer of cookbooks, John Russell. In his *Boke of Nurture*, Mr. Russell said: "Take shrympes, and seth hem in water and a litull salt, and lete hem boile ones or a litull more. And serve hem forthe colde: And no maner sauce but vinegre."

So things haven't changed much, after all, in the matter of cooking boiled shrimp, or shrympes.

The Ever-Lovin',
Blue-Eyed Scallop

I CAUGHT A SCALLOP ONCE IN BOGUE SOUND. IT WAS SICK. IT HAD
pretty blue eyes—a whole slew of them—all around the inside
of its shell, and I felt so sorry for it that I put it back in the

water, where it moved away by closing its shell with a jerk, so that the expulsion of water propelled its body forward a few feet. Only a few feet, because it was a sick scallop, suffering—probably—either from pollution, a bad percentage of salinity in the water, or merely old age.

The scallop has a pretty shell and all those exotic blue eyes, but he is, basically, an unfortunate creature in that he enters his senility in his second year. A two-year-old scallop is an old beggar, and a thirty-month scallop is a veritable patriarch. The scallop I found in Bogue Sound may well have been an antique two-year-old with a degenerating adductor muscle, a thickening shell, and sluggish reflexes.

Once upon a time, the scallop was an important variety of seafood in North Carolina. In 1928, North Carolina topped all other states in the production of scallop meat, but then the industry came upon evil times. A blight began to kill eel grass along the coast, and the hurricane of '33 did more damage. Production dropped from 686,220 pounds in 1929 to 91,458 pounds in 1934, and the industry has never recovered. The rather skimpy North Carolina supply of scallops has, at times, been further depleted by severe freezing weather catching the scallops on flats or in shoal water.

Because the scallop is not an important commercial species, perhaps, there hasn't been much money spent in trying to find out what killed the eel grass back in the '30's or what connection eel grass has with scallops anyway. About all we know is that scallops seem to like eel grass. When the eel grass went, so did the scallops; and when it comes back, you find a few scallops. That is, you find a few scallops in a fairly narrow area mostly in Carteret County in Core Sound and in the western end of Bogue

Sound. There are, or have been in the past, a few scallops in other northern areas of the state, especially around Ocracoke and Hatteras.

When I was doing my beaching around Morehead City I tried to find out about scallops, and about all I ever learned was that they were fairly scarce but that some people did gather them here and there. The "here and there" was guarded jealously, like a favorite fishing hole. I used to ask one of the top fresh-water fishermen in an inland area where he caught his beautiful bass, and he'd say, "Out behind the barn." Since we lived in the heart of a rather large town, that was, clearly, an evasive answer; and that's the kind of answer I would get as a tenderfoot when I asked old-time Bogue Sounders where they caught scallops.

I can, with some confidence, give this advice about finding scallops. If you see scallop shells along the shore of the sound, dead shells, then there must be live ones somewhere nearby. Doesn't that make sense? And I've been told, via the printed word and otherwise, that there are several ways to gather them. I would like to try one suggestion made by Euell Gibbons, a man who knows all about wild asparagus and things. Mr. Gibbons said, in his most recent book, that he stalked the blue-eyed scallop from a boat with a glass-bottomed box, looking down to the bottom through clear water.

If one could find clear water in an area where dead scallop shells litter the shore, then I believe the box with a view idea would work. Of course, not even Mr. Gibbons is infallible, since he also says that a soft-shell crab is soft for "a few days"; but, as I say, we're dealing with a field in which there is room for much detailed study, and no one man can know everything about everything.

What authorities there seem to be on scallops say that the bay scallop—that's a type of scallop that likes shallow, inshore waters—can grow to a three-inch diameter during its first year. Scallops prefer water with a touch more salinity than is generally found in good oyster waters.

My diligent research also tells me that the scallop shell has been used as a religious symbol and as a trademark for a major oil company. The scallop has added a descriptive word to the language. A scalloped edge is an edge made of a continuous series of half circles and a scalloped casserole has nothing to do with "a marine bivalve mollusk having the shell radially ribbed and the edge undulated."

In restaurants along the coast, the scallop is a part of most seafood platters. However, the scallops are generally imported from farther north, where the scallop industry is big. Further, most scallops found on restaurant menus are sea scallops which have been dredged from depths ranging from four to sixty fathoms. Northeasterners are more familiar with and more fond of the scallop than are most Southerners. Restaurant operators tell me that when scallops are ordered as the main attraction on a platter, the customer is usually a visitor from the North. For some reason the average native wants his scallops mixed with fried oysters, shrimp, and fish.

I've asked several restaurant men, and they all stoutly deny that they have ever served skate wing for scallops; but they all say that they've heard it has been done here and there.

Although there are several types of scallops up and down the East Coast, only two types are fished commercially. From the Bay of Fundy south through New England, dredgers take sea scallops. Off Massachusetts, the Georges Bank alone produced 15,000,000 pounds of scallop meat in one year.

The bay scallop is the one that offers a challenge to those who want to gather their own scallops. Back in the good old days a man with a scallop rake, which is somewhat like a potato digger with a small wire basket attached to hold the scallop, could harvest eight to fifteen bushels of bay scallops a day. Needless to say, things have changed. However, where conservation laws allow, some scallops can be taken by raking or by spying on the bottom with the aforementioned glass box, picking up the scallops with a long-handled net. It should also be fun to chase scallops with face mask and flippers, thus doing battle with the original jet-propelled creature in his own element. Wading might even yield a few scallops in the right area.

Scallops are not hard to open. Since they're swimmers, they tend to try to swim away, even after being taken out of the water, by opening their valves and snapping them shut. Thus they lose all their water and grow weak. The usual method of cleaning is to insert a sharp, thin knife, cut one side of the adductor muscle, open the shell, and throw away all but the strong, white muscle. A bushel of large scallops will yield about a gallon of muscle meat.

There is a lot of waste when one eats only the muscle of a scallop. Euell Gibbons, for one, states that the entire scallop may be eaten after being mealed and fried as one would fry an oyster. The waste part of a scallop also makes good bait for bottom-feeding fish such as croaker, gray trout, and blackfish.

There are, in addition to the usual bay and sea scallops, other varieties to be found in the mid-Atlantic coastal area. All scallops are edible. Some are just so small that it isn't commercially feasible to shuck them out. However, if you should ever run into quantities of the small calico scallop which grows only to about two inches in diameter, don't hesitate to use them, either whole or by extracting the adductor muscle.

As is the case with most shellfish, scallops can be eaten raw. However, those who recommend this practice eat only the muscle with, perhaps, a bit of melted butter for sauce.

Fresh scallops should be relatively odorless and should be rather creamy in color, instead of being very white.

The sparsity of my personal knowledge of scallops makes this a brief chapter. You can't go out and capture a mess of scallops just anywhere and, for those in an area where there is a supply of scallops, personal exploration will yield, I'm sure, a far greater store of knowledge.

Fried Scallops

Scallops	*Salt and pepper*
	Mealing mixture

Sprinkle washed scallops with salt and pepper. Roll in mealing mixture and deep fry at 375° until brown, or skillet fry in fat until brown. Drain on paper towels. Serve with a sauce of your choice.

Creamed Scallops

1½ pints scallops	*2 cups milk*
4 tablespoons butter	*1 tablespoon lemon juice*
4 tablespoons flour	*1 teaspoon onion, grated*
1 teaspoon salt	*1 tbsp. parsley, chopped*
Pepper to taste	*½ teaspoon dry mustard*

Make a white sauce by melting butter in saucepan and adding flour, salt, and pepper. Blend. Remove from heat and stir in milk. Cook, stirring constantly, until smooth. Add lemon juice,

onions, parsley, and mustard. Pour scallops into mixture and
heat to boiling point.

Scallops and Wine

1½ *pints scallops*   1 *small onion, chopped*
White wine   ½ *teaspoon parsley, chopped*

Place scallops, onions, and parsley in saucepan and cover with
wine. Simmer for three to five minutes, or until scallops are
white. Drain and serve with a sauce of your choice. Or drain,
chill, and serve over orange sections in a cocktail glass, topped
with a sauce or dressing of your choice.

Waiter, Bring Me Shad Roe

I KNOW APPROXIMATELY AS MUCH ABOUT COOKING FISH ROE AS I know about the nuclear generation of electricity—which accounts for the shortness of this chapter. All I know about the second subject is that a large power company has, at this writing, begun preliminary work on the construction of a nuclear generating plant in Brunswick County. At the risk of being branded as one who is averse to progress and of being run out of town by all the Jaycees, Boosters, businessmen, realtors, members of the Resources and Development Board, and landowners who think the new plant will double land values on sandy tracts which already have an asking price comparable to prime Florida citrus land, I will state in a small, hushed voice that I am not one hundred per cent thrilled by the prospect of having a nuclear reactor for a neighbor.

Perhaps the only people who agree with me are old settlers who were run off their land by the relentless force of "progress." When the generating plant is built, some of the prettiest riverside country in southeastern North Carolina will be closed to future residential or recreational development. Much prime riverfront is already occupied by the Sunny Point Army Ocean Terminal, where big union stevedores make more money loading bombs onto ships than is earned by most college presidents. I'm sure the union, the landowners, the merchants, and those who will work at the new generating plant would not agree with my contention that bombs and atomic reactors should be placed in areas where there would be less loss of natural beauty.

I am an unreconstructed nature lover. I think the flowering dogwood trees on the little highway between Southport and Wilmington are preferable to the neat fences along the new superhighways. I prefer the wildness of Bald Head Island to the glitter of Miami Beach. And it isn't just the alteration of the countryside that worries me about this thing we call progress. I have my doubts about all the assurances that the operation of a nuclear power plant on the Cape Fear will not have an adverse effect on the marine life of the river. I may be an alarmist; but I'm going on record so that later, if the worst happens—and it usually does—I'll be able to stand up and say I told you so.

I am told, by those who should know more about it than I do, that North Carolina's program to keep industry from polluting the air and the water is more strict and more successful than programs in many states. This should give me confidence. But when the wind is from the northwest, I can smell the pollution of the paper plant a full forty miles away, and I can't eat the oysters that are growing fat in the saltwater creek in my back yard because of sewage in the Cape Fear. When I read of the fatal pollution of the Great Lakes outside of large cities such as Chicago and Gary, I think back to that assuring statement about North Carolina's antipollution program and wonder just how relative it is. I remember news headlines of July, 1968, which told of a total fish kill over a twenty-mile stretch of the northeast Cape Fear River because of an accidental spill of industrial waste; and I wonder if we have to accept an anti-pollution program that is merely *more* strict and *more* successful than others. Other antipollution programs have failed completely. Where does that leave us?

Instances of improvement in an ecology through man's meddling are few and far between. Usually, when man applies his hand to a natural system, the result is disaster for nature.

If I had my say, I'd say let's not start changing the ecology of the Cape Fear River until we understand it better. Let's find out why blue crabs are scarce, why they have been dying in large numbers. Let's know what we're doing before we dump millions of gallons of heated water into a river.* Let's be sure that the minor change in water temperature that results won't

---

*Present plans reportedly call for releasing heated water from the nuclear generator directly into the Atlantic in the vicinity of one of my favorite gray trout holes.

—and this is merely wild supposition—encourage a population explosion of some minute organism which will usurp the place of an organism or creature with an important place in the food chain that ends in a nicely baked trout on the table. I'm no real authority on marine ecology, and I know very little about nuclear generating plants; but I know that to have fish roe—see, you thought I'd forgotten the heading of this chapter—you gotta have fish.

In the North Carolina coastal area, shad and mullet are the most common sources of fish roe, shad roe being the more familiar. More use could be made of the roe of the big, fat September mullet; and in the proper season, the lowly menhaden is a fine producer of delicious roe.

Generally, cooks recommend that fish roe, with the exception of small shad roe, be parboiled before broiling, creaming, baking, or frying. This is merely the first step in cooking roe. However, a fairly decent sandwich may be prepared from cold boiled roe and mustard, with a touch of lemon juice.

Parboiling Roe

To one quart of water, add one tablespoon of vinegar and one tablespoon of lemon juice and bring to a boil. Wash roe and submerge in boiling water. Simmer for five to ten minutes, according to size of roe. Drain roe and remove outer membrane.

Broiled Roe

Put parboiled roe into greased pan. Baste with melted butter and lemon juice. Sprinkle with salt and pepper. Broil under moderate heat about ten minutes, or until brown. Turn once or twice and baste during broiling.

Fried Roe

Roll parboiled roe in mealing mixture and fry in light oil about ten minutes, or until brown and done through.

Creamed Mullet Roe

Mullet roe	2 tablespoons flour
½ cup white wine	½ cup cream
2 tablespoons butter	2 egg yolks
1 teaspoon onion, chopped	Salt and pepper

Cover mullet roe with boiling water. Add wine and one-fourth teaspoon salt. Simmer for ten to fifteen minutes. Drain and remove membrane from roe. Mash roe. Melt butter in skillet and add onions. Cook for five minutes. Add roe. Stir in flour and cream. When hot, remove from heat and stir in egg yolks. Season with salt and pepper. Pour into shallow baking dish and broil under moderate heat about five minutes, or until top is brown.

NOTE: Creamed mullet roe is often used as a garnish for baked mullet. If used in this way, pour creamed roe over mullet which has been baked about fifteen minutes. Broil until brown.

Baked Shad and Creamed Roe

Baked shad	½ cup light cream
Shad roe	2 egg yolks, beaten
3 tablespoons butter	1 tablespoon lemon juice
1 teaspoon onion, grated	Salt and pepper
1½ tablespoons flour	1 cup buttered crumbs

Parboil roe, drain, and remove membrane. Mash. In skillet, heat butter and add onions and flour. Stir in cream and heat until thick. Add egg yolks while stirring. Add lemon juice and salt and pepper to taste. Spread roe over shad, sprinkle with buttered crumbs, and brown under broiler.

Fried Pogy Roe

Pogy roe	1 *beaten egg*
Salt and pepper	2 *teaspoons canned milk*
	¼ cup cornmeal or flour

Sprinkle roe with salt and pepper. Dip in egg-milk mixture and roll in flour or cornmeal. Fry in deep fat at 375° about five minutes, or until brown, or fry in shallow fat until brown.

NOTE: Locally, pogy roe is cooked without parboiling.

Pogy Roe and Eggs

Roe from two pogies	6 *eggs*
1 *tablespoon bacon drippings*	*Salt and pepper*

Mash roe and fry lightly in bacon drippings about three minutes. Add eggs and scramble until eggs reach desired consistency. Salt and pepper to taste.

Foil-Baked Roe

Fish roe (mullet, shad, or	*Lemon juice*
pogy roe)	*Parsley, minced*
Melted butter	*Salt*

Parboil roe, drain, and remove membrane. Small shad or pogy roe may be used without parboiling. Brush roe with melted butter. Put in buttered foil and sprinkle with lemon juice, parsley, and salt. Wrap and bake at 400° about ten or fifteen minutes.

Roe with Toast

Fish roe (six portions)   Parsley, minced
Flour   Salt and pepper to taste
1 cup butter   Lemon juice

Parboil if roe is large. Dip roe in flour and roll in butter to coat
well. Poach in butter in covered pan for ten minutes for raw roe,
or until brown for parboiled roe. Turn and sprinkle with parsley.
Cook for ten more minutes for raw roe, or until brown for parboiled roe. Season with salt and pepper and lemon juice. Place
on toast and pour butter from cooking pan over top.

Fish Stew, Mussel Chowder, and Other Oddities

MY FATHER-IN-LAW WAS AGAINST THE IDEA OF HIS DAUGHTER marrying an Oklahoma foreigner; but he finally paid the preacher and, after the inevitable had happened, accepted it with good grace. I think he even forgave me after a few years. At least, he took me fishing.

I had grown up in Oklahoma in the days before the huge dams were built—giving the Midwest as much or more shore-line than the eastern and western seaboards combined—so my fishing had been done in "tanks," farm ponds built by throwing up dirt dams across gullies. You could expect to catch monster perch, weighing up to four ounces, and fighting catfish, which might go half a pound.

I knew my new father-in-law was a great sportsman, and I was looking forward to some real fishing with him. I could picture myself sitting in a fighting chair, strapped in, a businesslike rod and reel in my hands, a big sailfish on the line, just walking on the water, dancing on his tail. When, a year or so after my marriage, I moved to North Carolina—partly because it was near an ocean of some size—my father-in-law took me fishing.

For catfish on the Cape Fear River.

Some of those fighting cats would go up to three-quarters of a pound. (There were yellow flies on the bank, chewing on me, that weighed almost as much as the fish.)

But we went fishing, and we caught catfish, and my father-in-law then proceeded to introduce me to his Famous Catfish Stew.

Later we did go fishing—what I call really fishing—for blues and mackerel, out of Morehead City, Sneads Ferry, and South-port, and for rockfish, in Town and Lilliput creeks. I caught a thirty-pound rockfish in Lilliput Creek at a spot too narrow to turn the boat around; and I got my share of blues and kings and Spanish, which we fried and baked and stewed and broiled; but the Famous Catfish Stew still holds a fine spot in my memory.

M.R.'s Famous Catfish Stew

A *few catfish, skinned*
A *can or two of corn*
A *can or two of English peas*
A *can or two of butter beans*
A *can of okra*
A *few potatoes, chunked*
A *few fresh tomatoes, chunked*
A *few carrots, sliced*
A *few stalks of celery, chopped*
3 *or 4 huge onions, chopped*
1 *clove garlic, minced*
About *half a bottle of Tabasco,*
   added every time someone
   decides the stew needs
   something
6 *or 8 fresh hot peppers, whole,*
   with seeds
Black *pepper added now and*
   then with a free hand

A *few dashes of chili pepper,*
   added when someone de-
   cides the stew still needs
   something
Cayenne *pepper, added by*
   one of the helpers who
   didn't see all the other
   pepper go in
Salt, *added by the cook,*
   passers-by, and the cook's
   wife, who is sure that the
   cook forgot the salt
A *couple of dashes of*
   Worcestershire
Anything *left in the refrig-*
   erator that the woman of
   the house wants to get
   rid of

Catfish stew is a holiday or weekend dish and is started—over cold beers—early in the afternoon, preferably outside. A large cast-iron cooking pot is preferable; but in an emergency almost anything, up to a small washtub, will do. Catfish stew is a community project and is not complete unless each bystander— and they seem to accumulate, after the first few beers—has contributed something to the stew. The directions are simple. Start putting things in the pot until you have everything you can think of in it. Start it boiling; then add water as necessary throughout the afternoon. The longer catfish stew is cooked, the better it seems to be. It's finished when, in the late or early evening, someone decides it's time to eat, or when the beer runs out. To nondrinkers, catfish stew is served with plenty of ice water or a fire extinguisher. And don't worry about the bones in the catfish. They have either been dissolved or been cooked out of the meat and settled to the bottom.

Actually, I'm doing my father-in-law's catfish stew a great injustice. Leave out most of the pepper, and it's a fine dish. I've seen the Famous Catfish Stew feed twenty or thirty people and inspire the dangedest sessions of community singing you've ever heard, with classics like "I've Been Working on the Railroad," "Give Me a Kitchen Mechanic," and "Ole Bucket-Mouth Mc-Ginty." And, the Famous Catfish Stew seems to linger on and on, improving with age, until you finally get down to the place where the bones have settled in the bottom and, reluctantly, you bury the remainder peacefully under a camellia bush in the back yard, because fish makes such good fertilizer.

For those who turn up their noses at the lowly catfish, saying he's a scavenger of the bottom of creeks and rivers, I can only ask, "When's the last time you had fried chicken?" Chickens don't all mature in antiseptic, scientifically controlled environments, you know. A lot of the chickens you buy on the market still scratch in the dirt of a crowded chicken yard.

In my nostalgic mood I've devoted, perhaps, too much space to the catfish. So, just to prove that this is still a seafood cookbook, let's get back to marine species with a few Brunswick County specials.

Mullet and Yams

Dressed or filleted mullet   1 *onion, chopped*
3 or 4 slices salt pork   *Sweet potatoes, peeled*
Salt and pepper

Render fat from salt pork and remove pork from pan. Fry onions in fat until tender. In heavy, covered iron pot, place alternate layers of sweet potatoes and mullet, adding salt and pepper. Put enough water in bottom of pot to make steam, but not enough to cover the first layer of fish. Pour onions and fat on top of final layer. Cover and cook until sweet potatoes are done and fish flakes easily.

Mullet Stew

3 *pounds fillet of mullet*	*Black pepper to taste*
2 *cans corn*	1 *tablespoon vinegar*
2 *cans tomatoes*	1 *or 2 onions*
2 *to 4 green peppers, chopped*	1 *stalk celery, chopped*
½ *teaspoon salt*	1 *can okra*
6 *to* 12 *potatoes, peeled*	

Put all ingredients except fish into pot and simmer for thirty minutes. Add fish and simmer until it is cooked to pieces. As in the case of any good chowder, repeated heatings improve the flavor.

Spot Stew

6 *whole dressed spots*	½ *teaspoon ground cloves*
2 *or* 3 *slices salt pork*	1 *teaspoon cinnamon*
1 *onion, chopped*	2 *teaspoons salt*
¼ *cup vinegar*	*Dash Tabasco*
2 *teaspoons sugar*	*Black pepper to taste*
Catsup or tomato paste	

Render fat from salt pork and remove pork from pan. Cook onions in fat until tender but not brown. Put spots over onions. Mix seasonings into catsup or tomato paste and cover fish with mixture. Simmer about twenty minutes, or until fish flakes when tested with a fork. May be served over rice with some of the sauce poured over all.

Poor Man's Stew

Picked crab meat, shrimp, or	2 or 3 slices fatback
bits of fish left over from a	2 or 3 potatoes, sliced
seafood dinner	1 onion, sliced

Salt and pepper to taste

Render fat from fatback in pot with cover and remove pork from pot. Place potatoes in fat, cover with onions, then with seafood particles. Put small amount of water in bottom of pot, cover, and cook until potatoes are done. Add salt and pepper.

Fish Chowder

2 pounds any fish, filleted	6 or more potatoes, diced
or bone in	2 carrots, diced
1 onion, chopped	½ teaspoon salt
2 or 3 slices salt pork	Black pepper to taste

Render fat from salt pork in pot with cover. Remove pork and add onions. Cook until tender. Add other ingredients, cover with water, and cook until vegetables are done. Fish should be cooked to pieces.

NOTE: Fish chowder may be made in any of the ways listed for clam chowder, with fish substituted for clams. Any fish may be used. Fillets are best; but small bone-in fish may be used, since the fish is cooked off the bones, which settle to the bottom of the pot.

Drunken Blackfish Chowder

4 lbs. blackfish, cut into slices	6 ¼ cups claret wine
2 to 4 slices fatback	3 cups water
1 to 2 onions, sliced	Salt and pepper
2 carrots, diced	2 tablespoons flour
2 garlic cloves, mashed	3 tablespoons butter
with salt	Juice of one lemon

In heavy iron pot, put fatback, onions, carrots, and garlic. Cook over low heat until soft. Put fish over vegetables and sprinkle with one-fourth cup claret wine. Cook until wine is evaporated. Pour in three cups claret and cook until wine is almost gone. Add three cups claret and three cups water. Add salt and pepper and cook about twenty minutes. Add flour and butter and cook about ten minutes, or until flour thickens. Add lemon juice and stir.

Snapper Chowder

4 pounds snapper (or other large fish)	1 garlic clove, minced
1 onion, sliced	1 teaspoon salt
1 cup carrots, diced	Black pepper to taste
1 cup potatoes, diced	½ lemon, sliced
	2 cups dry white wine

Place fish over vegetables in pan. Add seasonings and top with lemon slices. Pour in wine along sides of pot. Add water to cover vegetables and steam with pot covered, adding water if necessary, until vegetables are done.

Crab Stew

1 *dozen cleaned crab bodies*   2 *or 3 slices fatback*
Salt and pepper   3 *or 4 potatoes, sliced*
Mealing mixture   1 *or 2 onions, sliced*
Boiling water

Salt and pepper crab bodies and roll in mealing mixture. Render fat from fatback in heavy pot and remove pork from pot. Add layers of crab, potatoes, and onions. Repeat. Pour boiling water down sides of pot, being careful not to rinse meal off crabs, until water reaches level of last layer. Cover and cook until potatoes are done.

Kingfish Half and Half

Kingfish steaks, fresh or   3 *or 4 slices bacon or fatback*
   frozen   1 *onion, chopped*
6 *medium to large potatoes*   *Salt and pepper*

Peel and dice potatoes. Cut skin from kingfish steaks and dice same size as potatoes, in equal amount. In large pot, render fat from bacon, remove bacon from pot, and chop. Fry onions in fat until tender. Add potatoes and cook until about half done. Add salt, pepper, fish, and bacon. Cook until potatoes begin to disintegrate. Serve with Cuban or French bread and a tossed salad.

NOTE: This is an excellent way to utilize frozen fish steaks. Dicing is easier if done before fish is completely thawed.

TURTLES

The diamondback terrapin used to be an important commercial item in North Carolina, and it was hunted almost to extinction during the nineteenth century. The diamondback lives in brackish and, occasionally, in fresh water. In 1926, diamond-backs brought about seventy-three dollars a dozen on the Boston market.

The big loggerhead turtle, which comes up on the beaches to lay its eggs during a full moon in June, has often been eaten. Old turtle eaters say that a good turtle butcher can make cuts of meat from a large loggerhead to match any cut of steak. So I say, if that's the picture, if the turtle just matches steak, let's eat steak and leave the old girls to come to the beach, lay their eggs, and swim back into the sea.

I saw a couple of huge loggerheads that had been killed, wantonly killed, on Long Beach, not for their meat, but just for the fun of killing something so large, apparently. I like turtles. I like turtles better than I like some people—namely, people who would kill a big loggerhead just for the experience. Loggerhead turtles are a vanishing breed. It's fun to go turtle hunting during a full moon in a warm month on a nice night. It's an interesting experience to find a big turtle on her nest and watch her lay the eggs and cover them with her awkward, instinctive, and utterly laborious movements. My sympathy goes out to the big beast who comes out of her natural element to try to fight the odds against the survival of her species.

Let's don't eat loggerheads.

There are other turtles around. Smaller types of sea turtle are taken in nets now and then. Quite frequently, when I'm fishing or marsh hen hunting, I see turtle heads protruding from the water of marshy creeks. I've never eaten turtle or even stalked a turtle with malice.

I once knew a lady who, when her children grew up and left home, fell heir to two turtles that had been purchased as aquarium pets. From the charming size of a quarter dollar, the turtles grew, over the years, to an impressive size and were kept in the bathtub of the spare bathroom. Another lady kept half a dozen large land turtles in a walled planter outside her living room window, and she said they made the most delightful pets. She would take them out of the planter now and then for a walk; and the turtles would follow her slowly and ponderously around the front yard, walking in single file.

But turtle soup is served in fine restaurants, and terrapin stew is said to be fine eating. There are a few old-timers who can catch a terrapin whenever they want one—sometimes by merely poling a boat around the marshes until they sight a turtle under the water. (Terrapin, incidentally, is an American term, usually applied to an edible species of turtle.)

I have only one turtle recipe, given to me by an aged resident of the upper North Carolina coast. I've never tried it. I don't even know what kind of sea turtle is used in the recipe, but I'd guess, maybe, the green turtle.

Sea Turtle Stew

Small turtle	2 onions, chopped
1 tablespoon soda	1 dozen or more large
Boiling water	potatoes, cubed
3 or 4 slices salt pork	Salt and pepper

Only the legs of the turtle are used. After cutting them away, pour boiling water over them and remove skin and nails of flippers. Rinse. Cook in water with soda for thirty minutes. Meanwhile, render fat from salt pork and remove pork from pot. Fry onions in fat until tender. Pulverize salt pork and add to onions. Add potatoes. Bone turtle legs, cut meat into pieces, and add to pot. Add water and seasonings, cover pot, and cook until potatoes are well done.

MUSSELS

The literature on mussels is rather scarce—which is another way of saying, "I don't know a heck of a lot about mussels."

Alphonse F. Chestnut, quoted by Harden F. Taylor in *Survey of Marine Fisheries of North Carolina*, says that ribbed mussels, also known as horse mussels, are steamed and eaten by "local people along the coast."

One very authoritative reference book says that members of the marine family Mytilidae—that's mussels—are often implicated as a cause of, gulp, "paralytic shellfish poisoning." The symptoms of this hellish-sounding malady are: nausea, numbness, and paralysis of the tongue, lips, and limbs; and, if poisoning is severe, "other organs might be involved." However, except in the most serious cases, the effects disappear within a few hours or days.

My friend Viv, who eats mussels—local mussels—says you can die of strangulation while eating caviar.

I don't know.

You find mussels on tidal flats or in salt marshes between the high- and low-water marks. As with clams and oysters, mussels should be taken only from unpolluted water. To keep from getting grit into the meat, mussel shells should be washed thoroughly, then opened either by steaming or with an oyster knife. Our native mussels are not the finest kind, as far as I can determine. The best one is *M. edulis*, the blue mussel, which is plentiful in Europe and, to some extent, on the Eastern Seaboard up New England way. Mussels—at least *M. edulis* and, therefore, by association, the ribbed mussel of North Carolina—contain all sorts of valuable nutrients such as riboflavin, iron, copper, calcium, and other minerals, and lots of vitamin A.

North Carolina mussels have meat of yellow-orange color and rich flavor, and they remain untried by ye cowardly author. The reference book says that mussels can cause paralytic shellfish poisoning only when they have been eating a species of plankton known as dinoflagellates; so I suppose, if you check to see that there are no dinoflagellates around, it's all right to eat mussels.

My lawyer says that the reader has now been sufficiently warned and that I can go ahead and talk about mussel fritters, which are a lot like clam fritters, people say.

Mussel Fritters

2 *cups ground or chopped*	½ *teaspoon salt*
mussels	1 *beaten egg*
2 *cups flour*	*Milk*

Mix ingredients, except mussels, with milk to consistency of pancake batter. Stir in mussels. Fry on hot griddle until brown.

Mussels are also eaten raw, stewed, and steamed. And there are dozens of fancy French recipes for mussels.

Here's one of them:

Mussel Chowder

1 *peck mussels*	1 *bay leaf*
Dry mustard	*Sprig parsley*
1 *cup white wine*	3 *tablespoons butter*
1 *garlic clove*	2 *cups light cream*
	Salt and pepper

Soak scrubbed, unshelled mussels in strong mixture of water and dry mustard for four hours. Remove mussels, discarding water-mustard mixture. Scrub mussels again and put in large covered pan with wine, garlic, bay leaf, and parsley. Steam, covered, until shells have opened and juices have run out. Remove mussels from shells. Strain stock into second pan and boil until half of the stock is evaporated. Add mussels and butter and heat until butter is melted. Add cream, salt, and pepper, and heat without boiling.

ON SAFER GROUND WITH OCTOPUS AND SQUID

Still being somewhat exotic, let's talk about squid and octopus. Both are readily available: octopus is caught in fish traps, usually in the fall; and squid is taken in shrimp nets. Both are widely used for fish bait, and both are eaten by a few people who have traveled widely or picked up the habit from those who have. Like skate and shark, squid and octopus are great favorites in some parts of the world but enjoy little favor in this country.

My handy reference book, which seems to be bent on frightening me today, points out that there have been fatalities from octopus bite—not because of the fierceness of the animal, but because some species have a venom which is secreted by their salivary glands.

And is the plural of octopus octopuses, octopodes, octopi, or what? My old desk dictionary lists octopuses as first choice; the newest Webster's Unabridged gives a choice between octopuses and octopi; and my handy-dandy reference book, also of recent vintage, speaks plurally of octopodes.

When I was a commercial fisherman, which wasn't for long— only for one autumn season after I had gotten the old "Beth" where she'd run without heating up to the boiling point and had plugged enough of the cracks to keep her afloat—my mate and I went out to sea on one of those rare days. Dreamers such as I, who think of the sea in romantic terms, see her as calm, with just enough of a gentle swell to let you know you're not on some inland lake. We dreamers think of cruises with the wind in our hair, the sun overhead, and the boat loafing along lazily with the sea comfortably on the stern, on the bow, or nonexistent. I still dream of sailing among the islands under a smiling tropical sun or of a long trip into the South Seas under a blue Pacific sky.

But those who come up from the islands—specifically a nice young couple who were through here just this spring on a beauty of a fifty-footer with a modified racing hull and tall, fine spars—say that, while sailing, getting three hours of uninterrupted sleep is a novelty. They say that the tropical seas spawn half a dozen squalls a day and that the calm, picture-book sailing day is a rarity. Paul (Lobo) Tollefson—an artist who was about to become a national topic before he died a few years ago, who was a cabin boy on sailing schooners making the Scandinavia-Australia run, who had master's tickets to take any ship anywhere in the world, and who had lived in the South Pacific—once dashed my boyish dreams of being a second Sir Joshua Slocum by telling me about having to fight a World War II Liberty ship through twenty-five straight days of gale force winds in the balmy South Pacific. Then I read the incredible account of Sir Ernest Shackleton's trip across the Straits of Magellan, with waves that were forty, or ninety, or some fantastic number of feet high.

Now, where the heck was I? Talking about a rare day on a blackfish trapping trip in the old "Beth." My mate, who was so strong that I called him Tarzan, knew even less about the sea than I did; so we were not surprised to find that the sea, on that rare September day, was as flat as a table. There wasn't even a ground swell. There was no wind, but it was cool enough that we didn't work up a sweat pulling traps. We hit a good rock first off and started hauling in blackfish to fill the fish boxes we had on deck. We carefully threw overboard all the pesky octopi because the slimy beggars wouldn't stay in the fish boxes but insisted on crawling all over the deck, their suction cups clinging, making it difficult for us to pick them up. When we told some of the old-timers on the hill about how we had been busy all day throwing back octopuses (I've decided to be impartial in the use of plural), they had a good laugh because octopodes were selling for fifteen cents a pound. Whether the octopi were being shipped out of the state for food or were being sold for fish bait, I'm not sure. But they were bringing more than small blackfish; so the next day, when the sea began to show its true nature, we fought three-foot waves, saved all our octopodes, and came home with the boxes sliding around over the deck and the sea kicking up on the stern as we crossed the bar so that the waves looked—I'm not swearing how high they actually were—as high as a telephone pole; and I began to understand how Shackleton felt, but without the cold. That came later.

But about octopussies.

HOW TO PREPARE AND COOK AN OCTOPUS

There seem to be two schools of thought on cleaning octopi. The simple way is to use the tentacles only. Just cut off the tentacles, chop them into one-inch pieces, and skin. Skinning is greatly facilitated by pouring boiling water over the pieces. If one wants to make use of some of the body parts, it is necessary to cut off the beast's head—which is there, all you have to do is look for it—then remove the mouth, with its parrot-like beak, and the innards of the octopus. Then cut the body portions into strips.

I'll tell you this: you gotta really *want* to eat octopus. After you have cut the meat into one-inch pieces, you beat the heck out of the pieces. Don't cut. Just beat. You can use, for lack of any other tool, the bottom of a Coke bottle; but don't get too fierce and break the bottle in your hand. If such a misfortune should happen, I'll say I told you so. Then, too, you'll have to wash the octopus again, for human blood is not a part of the recipe.

But we're beating the pieces of octopus to break down the tough tissue. The bigger the octopus, the tougher he is; so stick with the small ones when possible.

The next step is to marinate the meat for twenty-four hours.

Mediterranean Style Marinade

1 *cup olive oil*	6 *peppercorns*
Bay leaves	*Juice of one or more lemons*
	Meat tenderizer (optional)

Mix ingredients in shallow container. Add small amount of meat tenderizer if desired.

Another Marinade Style

1 *cup dry white wine*	1 *teaspoon celery salt*
1 *teaspoon Worcestershire*	*Dash garlic salt*
Dash of oregano	*Juice of one or more lemons*
1 *teaspoon salt*	*Meat tenderizer (optional)*
	Dash Tabasco (optional)

Mix ingredients in shallow container. Add small amount of meat tenderizer if desired. Tabasco may also be added, if a touch of hot is welcomed.

Grilled Octopus

Octopus tentacles, cut into one-inch slices
Mediterranean Style Marinade

Prepare octopus as directed above. Marinate in Mediterranean Style Marinade in a shallow bowl or dish for twenty-four hours. Cook on skewers about four inches from seasoned firebed of charcoal for five minutes per side, or until tender.

Boiled Octopus

2 *lbs. octopus, cut into chunks*	1 *tablespoon parsley, minced*
1 *onion, chopped*	*Dash or two of oregano*
1 *clove garlic, chopped*	1 *or 2 bay leaves*
½ *cup olive oil*	1½ *cups white wine*
1 *tbsp. celery leaves, chopped*	*Juice of one lemon*

Prepare octopus as directed and marinate for twenty-four hours in either of the octopus marinades listed. Put onions, garlic, and olive oil in cooking pot and cook until onion is tender but not brown. Add octopus chunks and other ingredients. Cover and simmer for at least two hours. Add water, a cup at a time, as needed.

SQUID

The squid is a bit more tender than the octopus. The meat tastes much like octopus and is described as being sweet and delicious. The squid I've seen on this coast usually run rather small, so that should be in their favor, flavor-wise, if one decides to use them for anything other than fish bait.

Squid are cleaned by simply pulling off the head. If this operation is performed properly, the internal organs will come out attached to the head; and all that remains to be done is to rinse the body of the squid thoroughly, making sure to remove all traces of the squid's inky fluid.

Baked Squid

2 *pounds squid*	½ *cup tomato paste*
Olive oil	½ *cup white wine*
1 *onion, chopped*	4 *or* 5 *cups cooked rice*
1 *clove garlic, minced*	*Juice of one lemon*

Braise squid in frying pan until liquid runs out of meat. Drain and dry. Fry in oil with onions and garlic until onions are tender. Add other ingredients, except lemon juice, and pour over bed of cooked rice in baking dish. Bake at 400° for twenty-five minutes. Add lemon juice before serving.

Fried Squid

Roll or shake squid in mealing mixture containing salt and pepper. Fry in small amount of fat or butter about ten minutes, or until brown. Serve with lemon juice or a sauce of your choice.

I'm told that there is a West Indian dish that features squid in ink. A traveler from the antique land of Puerto Rico said that after one has eaten the inky mixture, his tongue is black for days. Then, too, I've heard about a Spanish way of frying squid.

One cuts the squid body tube into rings and fries the slices as one would fry onion rings. Sounds fine to me. I'd guess that an egg-milk moistening base and a roll in flour or meal would help; and it might be best to fry the little squid rings in butter.

ROASTED PERIWINKLES, ANYONE?

Anyone who has ever been out in a salt marsh has probably noticed the plentiful little snails climbing on the marsh grass. When a marsh-hen-hunting boat is being poled through grass, the snails are often dislodged and fall into the boat, where they die and make a disgusting smell.

Wal, friends, I found out, from a couple of handy reference books, that them furriners over thar in Europe eat them little snails.

Yep. The common periwinkle. That little ole snail. They grow about one-half inch long, but the books say that tons of them are roasted and sold from pushcarts in the streets of European cities. Like peanuts. I don't know the exact procedure, and the handy reference books don't go into detail. All I know is that they are roasted. Then, I suppose, one eats them like pistachio nuts, although breaking the shell might be tough on the teeth.

I'm not recommending roasted periwinkles, even if Rhode Island did produce over a hundred thousand pounds for commercial use in 1945. (My handy reference book isn't quite up to date on that point.) I merely include this bit of fantastic information to let the reader know that I know it.

One more item regarding periwinkles. Our native, or imported, periwinkles—some books say they were introduced to this country from Europe—are smaller than the French species, which grow as long as one and a half inches. The French, in addition to roasting periwinkles, boil them in heavily salted water and pick out the loosened meat to eat with butter or a sauce or to use in making periwinkle soup.

I would guess that periwinkles, small as they are, could be used as the flavoring agent in a chowder, just as the tiny coquina is used in chowders and soups. The little coquina, a species of clam, has been gathered in marketable quantities in Florida. Perhaps something money-making could be done with the periwinkles. Anyone who wants to go into the periwinkle business is invited to get in touch with the author, who will, for a fee— say fifty per cent of profits—allow periwinkles to be picked from his front lawn, which is a salt marsh stretching a mile or so to the Intracoastal Waterway.

SURF CLAMS, COCKLES, AND SEA URCHINS

Among the many things I don't know is how to get surf clams. They make good eating, according to all the information I have. They are very sandy, however, and have to be washed thoroughly.

Something else I don't know is how to get cockles. Their shells are common on the strands, and Sweet Molly Malone always went around singing "Cockles and mussels, alive, alive, oh." In the New England area, cockles have been taken in commercial quantities.

And since I'm in a confessing mood, I'll own up to my lack of information about sea urchins. In some of the Mediterranean countries, such as Italy and southern France, a certain species of sea urchin is a delicacy. The white-spined sea urchin is eaten by natives of the West Indies, also. On our West Coast, people must know how to eat sea urchins, because I saw a character on the Walt Disney show having sea urchin for lunch. I have heard that Italians on the West Coast eat the red urchin raw

and say that it has a more subtle flavor than caviar. It seems
that eating sea urchin is sorta sexy, since it is the roe or repro-
ductive glands that are used for food. Most sea urchins have
poison glands, but they are rarely venomous enough to be a serious threat.

Salting, Pickling, Smoking, and Stuff

MY WIFE PLANTED FLOWERS IN ALL MY SALT-FISH BUCKETS. THE buckets are made of white oak or some similar wood, like the old wooden barrels, and they used to have wooden tops. The

flowers are dying, though, either because I overfertilized them or because we didn't wash out all the brine.

I suppose someone, somewhere, still makes buckets for salting fish, but I'm ignorant of the vital facts. Fish-salting is a thing of the past, mostly, except for a few people who actually savor the taste of salt mullet or spot or mackerel.

In the days before prosperity afflicted this country and convinced a good portion of the populace that one hundred dollars a week is a poverty wage, salting fish for the winter made good sense. Salt fish was better than no fish at all, as the menhaden crew members said about salt menhaden; and there was sort of a tang to salt fish that seemed to go with winter morning breakfasts.

I know of only one person who regularly salts fish now. I'm sure that there are more because I don't know everyone along the coast, but in my circle of acquaintance there's only one bucket of corned mullet or spot outside the kitchen door in the cold air on a frosty fall morning. It's just too easy to put fish away in the deep freezer.

Smoking fish and pickling oysters are also, seemingly, dying arts. I confess to never having encountered a pickled oyster; but I've patronized a local establishment which, one fall, featured smoked spot and cold beer, and the combination was pretty good.

The processes presented in this chapter are largely untested by the writer, but they are, nevertheless, tried and true, since they have been gathered painstakingly from those who have smoked, corned, and pickled for a long time. I can testify that corned mullet is fittin', right tangy when properly prepared with pepper and vinegar and served with grits.

I've never been able to determine how the term "corning"

became associated with salting fish or meat. I don't question the use of the word "corn" any more than I question some old skipper when he says he's going to "cork" his boat, meaning that he's going to caulk the seams and butts of the hull. It's just one of those things that you couldn't fight if you wanted to, so I'll use the term "corn" just as if I knew exactly where it came from.

Corned Mullet

Filleted mullet   *Noncorrosive container (such*
Noniodized salt   *as wood, glass, porcelain,*
                               earthenware, etc.)

Put a large amount of salt in a shallow pan. Roll fillets in salt and layer in container, sprinkling liberally with salt as layers are built up. Store in cool place, covered against insects and dust, for two weeks. Pour off accumulated liquid. Mix salt with fresh water until the brine will float an egg, and pour over fish to cover. Fish will now keep indefinitely.

CORNED SPOTS AND MACKEREL

Spots are usually not filleted for corning but are sliced down the back to expose more flesh to the salt. The process is the same as in the case of corned mullet. Mackerel are corned, but rarely, in fillets or steaks.

COOKING CORNED FISH

One method of cooking salt fish is simply to soak it, skin up, in fresh water overnight, then fry it as you would fry fresh fish. Salt fish for breakfast are usually boiled in a small amount of water, seasoned with pepper and vinegar, and served with eggs and grits.

Salt Fish Cakes

1 *pound salt mullet*	¼ *teaspoon celery seed*
Paprika	2 *to 4 tablespoons flour*

Soak corned fish overnight. Boil about ten minutes. Grind in meat grinder. Mix with seasonings and flour, form into patties, and fry on hot griddle until brown.

Dried Herring

Mix brine strong enough to float an egg. Clean herring and remove head and stomach. Soak in brine for three days. Remove and hang up to dry. Fish should keep for several months. To cook, soak overnight in water, skin, and fry or boil.

Pickled Oysters

2 *pints oysters*	1 *tablespoon black pepper*
1 *quart vinegar*	1 *teaspoon mace*
1 *tablespoon whole cloves*	1 *tablespoon butter*

Strain liquid from oysters. Add vinegar to liquid and heat. Add spices and boil. Add oysters and return to boil. Add butter. Store in cool place and serve cold.

SMOKING FISH

When the Army had a Navy in Southport, we knew a girl of Spanish-American origin who got CARE packages. At the time, one couldn't buy tequila in North Carolina ABC stores, at least not in those in our area. Our Latin friend would get tequila through the mail in Clorox bottles. These plastic bottles have been used for a lot of things. With the cap on, they make good floats for nets or good markers for traps. Cut into a scoop shape, they are fine for bailing out a boat. And cleaned and capped, they make good shipping containers for tequila. (If the postal authorities read this, I'll swear that this portion of the book is fiction and fiction only.)

Actually, the most important part of the CARE package was not the tequila, although a good Mexican meal is naught without a slug of the cactus juice to instill appetite, but the chili peppers, the homemade hominy, and the jerky. Our friend's parents thought she was marooned a long way from civilization, and they took care of her, even sending, once, a wash basin so that she'd be able to take a bath. They sent pinyon nuts and fried beans and the ingredients for *posole* and other fine Mexican dishes.

What has this to do with drying fish by smoke? Not much, except that venison jerky tastes a bit like a properly smoked fish. Jerked meat is first cut into thin strips and then dried in the sun with a bit of salt. Smoked meat is dried in heat and smoke, with the smoke adding a flavor which, unlike the flavor of jerked meat, is not a rawish taste.

Because the flavor of smoked fish is something special, the art of smoking is preserved in many localities along the coast. Almost any fish of the lean category can be smoked; but the smaller the fish, the better he cures in smoke, so the spot is a favorite fish to use. To smoke larger fish, such as September mullet or mackerel, it is necessary to fillet the fish and then strip it. With the spot, it is necessary only to clean it.

In preparation for smoking, the fish are scaled, then eviscerated, head on. After the stomach contents have been removed and the strong-tasting stomach flaps cut away, the gills are removed with a sharp knife. Spots may be smoked without the head; but it seems to be customary to smoke them head on so that the eye socket may be used as a hanger. Brine is mixed strong enough to float an egg, and the fish are soaked in it for twelve hours. Then they are put in a smokehouse and smoked over hickory or other nutwood smoke for twelve hours.

Fish-smokers say that a green nutwood is mandatory for smoking. No substitutes are allowed. Hickory is best; oak is acceptable. Pecan or walnut may be used, although not many people would want to cut down a good pecan or walnut tree just to smoke a fish.

THE SMOKEHOUSE

The smokehouse is an outhouse-sized contraption with a door and a dirt floor. Scrap lumber of any type may be used to build a house 4 x 4 feet, with a slanted roof six feet high on the low side and seven feet on the high side. The house should not be airtight but should be fairly close without sealing.

Inside the house, fish-hangers made from pieces of 2 x 2 are suspended, like the slats of a bed, from boards nailed at the ends of the house near the top. Stainless steel nails are driven through the 2 x 2's to hold the fish. The spots to be smoked are hung on the fish-hangers with the nails through the eye-sockets of the fish. Fish strips are merely impaled on the nails.

The fire is started on the dirt floor of the smokehouse with charcoal or wood or both. When a good bed of coals is built up, green nutwood is laid on the coals and the smokehouse door is closed. Green hickory or oak on top of a good bed of coals, with not too much air to breathe, will smoke and smoke; and that's the idea. The fish shouldn't be too close to the fire; it shouldn't be cooked by the heat. The idea is to let the fish soak in the smoke for about twelve hours, or until the smoke and the salt from the brine have cured the fish into a tasty, fairly dry goodness.

Of course, twelve hours is a long time; but if the fish are rather large, it may take a bit more than twelve hours to get them right. The best thing to do is to have a party, a fish-smoking party. Then everyone takes turns checking on the fish to see if the wood is smoking properly and has not burned away.

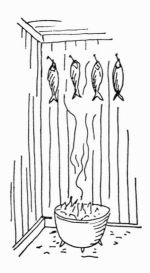

A bit of bay wood added to the smoking fire helps the flavor of smoked fish, but it shouldn't be overdone—a stick or two now and then throughout the twelve-hour period is enough. And to give the smoked fish a golden brownness that adds to the flavor, the fire should be cooled, when it gets too hot, with dark Karo syrup. The syrup is poured right on the hot coals when they begin to burn more than smoke.

A smoked fish will last a few days in the refrigerator, but

smoking is not a long-term preservative. Smoked fish freeze well when airtight containers are used and may be thawed in the refrigerator or at room temperature. A stock of smoked fish in the freezer assures party snacks and quick meals without much ado.

Gilding the Lily—A Reluctant Chapter on Sauces

I BELIEVE THAT HIGHLY-SEASONED, SAUCE-COVERED DISHES WERE developed by cooks who lacked refrigeration facilities and were forced to disguise the taint of overripe meat. I think it fringes on sacrilege to foul the basic flavor of a good fish, and the mere mention of a sauce among seafood lovers can start an argument. However, there are many ingenious ways of disguising the flavor of fish and other seafoods for those who feel that this is a necessary part of being civilized.

There are many commercially packaged seafood sauces. Most of them contain horseradish, which I cannot abide. For a simple, no-nonsense, homemade seafood sauce, which I call Dab Sauce, the basic ingredients are catsup, Worcestershire, and a hot sauce. I use Tabasco, but any other hot sauce can be substituted. It's all a matter of individual taste. If you like horseradish, put in a dash. If you like the tartness added by a dash of lemon juice, fine. You're the one who is going to eat it.

Dab Cocktail Sauce

Catsup   *Worcestershire*
                              Tabasco

Pour a couple of dabs of catsup into an individual container. Add a dash of Worcestershire and a dash of Tabasco to taste.

Personally, I think that most of the concoctions I have included in this chapter have inland origins. They are rarely seen, at any rate, along the unsophisticated lower coast. I've picked the recipes up, here and there, from cooks who speak good English and wear expensive clothing; and I've stolen some of them from various uncopyrighted publications. Some of the recipes, such as the continental monstrosity that is called *A Buerre Noir* or—gah—black butter, I include mainly for their comedy value. If someone served some of the following sauces to me, I'd be sure that he was trying to utilize three-day-old fish by killing the strong, stale taste with various glops.

A Buerre Noir
(A Ver' Famous Conteeneental Deesh)

4 *tablespoons butter*   ½ *cup vinegar*

Brown butter in saucepan *without burning*. Add vinegar while
butter is hot. (Careful of splattering butter!) Pour over fish
while both fish and sauce are hot. Entire mess may then be fed
to cat, if he'll eat it.

There are some sauces or relishes that are more sensible. Here
are a few old standards:

Tartar Sauce
1
1 *cup mayonnaise*   1 *tbsp. mixed pickles, minced*
1 *tablespoon onion, minced*   1 *tablespoon parsley, minced*
              1 *tbsp. capers (if available)*
Mix all ingredients and chill.

2
½ *cup mayonnaise*   1 *tablespoon parsley, minced*
1 *tbsp. green olives, minced*   1 *tablespoon pickles, minced*
              1 *tablespoon onion, minced*
Mix and chill.

Lemon Sauce
1
1 *teaspoon lemon juice*   3 *tablespoons butter*
              Black pepper to taste

Melt butter. Mix in lemon juice and black pepper. Serve hot.

2

1 *teaspoon lemon juice*   3 *tablespoons butter*
Tabasco to taste

Melt butter. Mix in lemon juice and Tabasco. Serve hot.

NOTE: A simple taste combination such as lemon juice and butter, with a touch of hot sauce of some kind, goes well with fish in its drier forms, such as large, baked steaks.

Cocktail Sauce

6 *tablespoons catsup*   4 *tablespoons lemon juice*
2 *tablespoons horseradish*   *Dash celery salt or garlic salt*
Tabasco to taste

Blend all ingredients and serve.

NOTE: Goes well with almost any fried or baked seafood, if one likes horseradish.

Hollandaise Sauce

3 *egg yolks, beaten*   ½ *teaspoon salt*
½ *cup butter*   *Black pepper to taste*
2 *tablespoons lemon juice*   ½ *cup boiling water*

Cream butter, add beaten egg yolks, and beat. Add lemon juice and seasonings. Pour in boiling water. Cook in double boiler until thick. Serve immediately. Good with baked fish.

Chili-Mustard Sauce

¼ *cup butter*   1 *teaspoon table mustard*
½ *cup onion, minced*   2 *tablespoons chili sauce*
1 *clove garlic, minced*   ½ *teaspoon salt*
1 *teaspoon Worcestershire*   *Black pepper to taste*

Mix butter, onions, and garlic. Cook over low heat until onions are tender, about ten minutes. Stir often. Add remaining ingredients, mix, and heat.

Green Onion Sauce

2 *green onions with tops, minced*	1 *teaspoon table mustard*
½ *cup salad oil*	1 *teaspoon dry mustard*
2 *tablespoons vinegar*	*Dash garlic salt*
	¼ *cup celery, chopped*

Mix ingredients. Let stand for at least an hour before serving. May be heated.

Cucumber Sauce

1 *cup whipping cream*	2 *tablespoons lemon juice*
½ *teaspoon salt*	½ *teaspoon onion juice*
⅛ *teaspoon cayenne pepper*	1 *cucumber, chopped*

Beat cream until thick. Add salt and cayenne pepper. Add lemon juice slowly. Fold in cucumber and onion juice. Chill.

Sauces That Are Almost Dishes by Themselves

Most of the following sauces are excellent for making a good meal of surplus seafood. Some may be used with leftover fish to make a delicious and economy-minded meal. Some may be served with noodles or rice. Some have no use that I know of and are included just because I know about them and am eager to flaunt my knowledge.

Green Pepper Sauce

2 *large green peppers*	1 *small can mushrooms*
1 *clove garlic*	1 *teaspoon Worcestershire*
1 *onion*	1 *teaspoon dry mustard*
4 *tablespoons bacon drippings*	*Dash cayenne pepper*
4 *cups canned tomatoes*	1½ *teaspoons salt*

Chop peppers, garlic, and onion and cook in bacon drippings until tender. Add tomatoes, mushrooms, and seasonings and cook slowly about twenty minutes, or until mixture thickens. May be served with almost any seafood and is delicious when poured hot over crumbled, boned, leftover fish.

Mushroom Sauce

1 *can cream of mushroom*	2 *tablespoons butter*
soup	1 *cup milk*
⅓ *cup onions, chopped*	½ *teaspoon salt*

Cook onions in butter in saucepan until golden. Stir in soup, then milk. Add salt and heat while stirring. Use as Green Pepper Sauce is used.

Tomato Sauce

2 *cups canned tomatoes*	1 *tsp. or less Worcestershire*
2 *tablespoons flour*	½ *teaspoon salt*
2 *tablespoons butter*	*Black pepper to taste*

Boil tomatoes about ten minutes, or until mushy. Strain through colander, forcing pulp of tomatoes through. Discard roughage. Melt butter, mix in flour, and add hot tomatoes and seasonings. Simmer until mixture reaches a pleasing state of thickness.

NOTE: This recipe is for use when you're caught without tomato paste or catsup in the house, and the good cook who gave it to me says it tastes better than a store-bought sauce.

Any of the fancy sauces listed may be used as the imagination dictates; but I wouldn't want to mess up fresh yellow-fin trout fillets with any of them. At the risk of being repetitious, I want to say that most of the sauces are excellent for making a good meal of leftovers. There's something about cooking fish or shrimp or other seafoods that goads the average woman into being extremely wasteful. Perhaps it's because, when fish are caught, they are sometimes caught in glorious plenty. When a fisherman comes home after a hard day's work over a lure and line with dozens of fish, it's easy to overestimate the amount of fish that will be eaten. Then there are leftover fish, and that's where some of the sauces come in.

Of course, the sauces may be combined with seafoods in a variety of ways. Some of them may be used to tone down the taste of strong fare such as whelks or horse mussels, and some of them make excellent dips for snack items such as prepared crab fingers.

An Handful of Meal
in a Barrel

MEALING COMES NATURALLY TO EXPERIENCED COOKS AND, SUR-
prisingly, gives all sorts of trouble to occasional cooks. Basically,
mealing is dipping the seafood in a liquid mixture, then rolling
it in a dry mixture in preparation for frying, either in deep fat

or in shallow fat. The liquid mixture is usually milk or canned milk, water, egg, or a combination of these ingredients. The dry mixture may be cornmeal, flour, bread or cracker crumbs, pancake flour, or a combination of these.

Mealing helps brown the fish and makes a slight crust on the outside. On small pieces of seafood, a large crust may be built up by repeated mealings—dipping in liquid mixture, then in dry mixture, and repeating as many times as desired.

Mealing with Cornmeal

Cornmeal   Salt and pepper
            Milk, water, or beaten egg

Mix cornmeal with salt and pepper. Dip fish in milk, water, or beaten egg. Roll in meal.

Mealing with Flour or Pancake Flour

Flour or pancake flour   Salt and pepper
            Milk, water, or beaten egg

Mix flour and seasonings in bowl, in clean paper bag, or in plastic bag. Dip fish in milk, water, or beaten egg. Roll in mealing mixture or drop into bag, close top of bag, and shake.

Mealing with Crumbs

½ cup bread crumbs or   Pepper to taste
    cracker crumbs   1 egg
½ teaspoon salt   2 teaspoons canned milk

Beat egg and blend in milk. Dip fish in egg-milk mixture and roll in crumbs to which seasonings have been added.

Mealing with Cornmeal and Flour

½ cup flour
¼ cup cornmeal (fine)
1 teaspoon paprika

¼ cup canned milk
1½ teaspoons salt
Pepper to taste

Combine flour, meal, and paprika. Combine milk, salt, and pepper. Dip fish in milk mixture. Roll in flour mixture.

Mealing for Deep-Fat Frying

¼ cup cornmeal or flour
½ teaspoon salt

Pepper to taste
1 egg

2 teaspoons canned milk

Beat egg and blend in milk. Dip fish in egg-milk mixture and roll in flour or cornmeal to which seasonings have been added.

For Those Who Like Bread

HUSHPUPPIES GO WELL WITH ANY SEAFOOD, AND WITH A LOT OF other foods, and are almost always served on seafood platters in restaurants on the North Carolina coast.

Aside from the fact that I'm not rich, nothing frustrates me more than my complete inability to make an edible hushpuppy. This is also the one area in which my wife, who has worked out rather successfully for some twenty-one years, is an abject failure. Any number of people I know make fine hushpuppies. My mother-in-law tosses them off, on the occasion of a family fish fry, with disgusting ease. Dozens of seafood restaurants along the coast make hushpuppies by the ton. My hushpuppies fall apart when dropped into deep fat; or they harden into unchewable, indigestible balls.

Cornbread from scratch, either baked or fried, is a bit less likely to go bad under the hands of this self-styled seafood cook; but it, too, is so unsure in results, so uneven in quality, that I sometimes give up in despair and use a box or two of Jiffy cornbread mix from the pantry shelf.

This may not sound too serious; but I'm an Oklahoma boy, brought up on cornbread and beans, cornbread and fried potatoes, cornbread and sweet milk. Jiffy is a fine product, and I suppose I consume as much of it as any single nonstockholder in the Jiffy company; but it's a commercialized, smooth, sweetened cornbread that just does not have the chewy ability to fight back—a quality that is important to a good cornbread, be it baked, fried, or in hushpuppy form.

Perhaps natural-born Southerners don't have my difficulties with hushpuppies and cornbread. Out West, we didn't put sugar in cornbread—not ever. And we never deep-fried it, as one does hushpuppies, but did, sometimes, fry it on a flat sheet over an open fire or in a greased skillet on the stove. As a Southerner both by ancestry and by choice, I sometimes feel that hushpuppies discriminate against me when they disintegrate as I try to cook them.

Good cooks—that is, cooks who understand cornbread—have their own little techniques; and while turning out good cornbread seems to be effortless for them, just ask them to tell you how to do it, and they suddenly become vague and start telling you about a pinch of this and a dab of that. And the problem is, they're not *trying* to make it difficult. It's just that you have to have a feel to make good cornbread, and all of my feeling about it seems to be concentrated in the ability to appreciate a good pone or a good hushpuppy.

I have collected at least a half-dozen hushpuppy recipes, and I refuse to guarantee any of them; for the very women who sat down with me and, after going through the little of this and dab of that stage, gave me a cup of this and a teaspoon of that information, then went into the kitchen, threw the carefully calibrated recipe away, and did it by feel. However, there are enough variations here to make a good point of departure into the adventure of making hushpuppies. Remember, I married my wife because I thought she could cook like her mother; but when I asked my mother-in-law for her cornbread recipe, this is what I got:

"Well, you take meal and a little bit of flour, not much if you want a little bit, more if you want more . . . ."

"But how much meal? How much flour?"

"Oh, well, maybe a cup of meal and a little bit of sugar."

"But what about the flour?"

"Well, you put the flour in, and mix it stiff, and drop it in about a teaspoon at a time."

After another half hour of this, after I'd hog-tied her to a chair and threatened her with a club, she came up with the following ingredients, which may work for you, too.

My Mother-in-Law's Hushpuppies with Milk and Onions

1 *cup meal*   1 *teaspoon sugar*
½ *cup self-rising flour*   2 *tablespoons onions, chopped*
¼ *teaspoon salt*   1 *egg*
                    About one cup milk

Mix dry ingredients and onions. Stir in egg. Add milk until mixture is stiff. Spoon into deep fat and cook at 375° until golden brown.

Hushpuppies with Beer and Onions

1 *cup meal*   1 *teaspoon sugar*
½ *cup self-rising flour*   2 *tablespoons onions, chopped*
¼ *teaspoon salt*   1 *egg*
                    About one small can of beer

Mix dry ingredients and onions. Stir in egg. Add beer until mixture is moderately stiff. (Mix should be slightly thinner than that made with milk.) Spoon into deep fat and cook at 375° until golden brown.

Three More Hushpuppy Recipes

1

1 *pound fine cornmeal*   *Pinch of soda*
1 *tablespoon salt*   1 *cup buttermilk*
1 *tablespoon sugar*   1 *egg*
                    Water

Mix dry ingredients and stir in buttermilk and egg. Add water to make thick mixture. Spoon into hot fat and cook at 375° for five to ten minutes, or until golden brown.

2

1½ *cups meal*   1 *teaspoon baking powder*
½ *cup plain flour*   ½ *cup sugar*
¼ *teaspoon salt*   1 *beaten egg*
                    Water

Mix dry ingredients. Add egg. Stir in water to make thick batter. Spoon into deep fat and cook at 375° until brown.

3

1½ *cups enriched cornmeal*   ½ *teaspoon salt*
½ *cup all-purpose flour, sifted* 1 *small onion, chopped*
2 *teaspoons baking powder*   1 *beaten egg*
1 *tablespoon sugar*   ¾ *cup milk*

Sift dry ingredients together. Add onions. Add egg and milk and stir. Spoon into hot fat and cook at 375° until brown.

So, you see, there's quite a variety of opinion about hushpuppies. Of the five recipes given, I prefer the first—perhaps because my mother-in-law's hushpuppies were the first I ever ate. The recipe using beer is a bit harder to handle because the hushpuppies tend to crumble more as they are dropped into the deep fat. Good, though.

Onions may be left out or added to any of the recipes, of course. However, I consider them necessary to any good hushpuppy.

Another thing about hushpuppies is that it's fine to cook them in the same deep fryer where you're cooking fish. In fact, you can cook fish, hushpuppies, and French fries all at once if you're working with a large deep fryer.

Most cooks handle hushpuppies easily. For those who, like

me, have trouble with them, here's one last suggestion: in a pinch, you can stop in at any seafood restaurant, where they always have hushpuppies ready, and buy a pound or so quite economically. I've been known to do just that to complete the menu for a fish fry.

CORNBREAD

There are other breads that go nicely with various seafoods. One of my all-time favorites is a delicious fried cake, demonstrated to me by Miss Bessie Stubbs, one of the finest seafood cooks I know. She says the secret is in using pancake flour. The bread is so good that it's almost a meal in itself. In fact, the night I ate it, we had nothing but fried cornbread and roasted oysters with a sauce; and it was, as the Southern saying goes, mighty fittin'.

In talking about cornbreads of all sorts, Miss Bessie told me something I've heard from a number of good cooks—that the meal is all-important. Everyone who has done much cooking with meal has a favorite brand, but Miss Bessie says that it should be ground medium or fine because coarse meal is good only for baking bread.

Unfortunately, this fried cornbread thing is about as touchy as hushpuppies, although I've been more successful with it. It might take a couple of tries for a complete greenhorn to learn how to handle it, but the effort is very much worth while.

Miss Bessie's Fried Cornbread

2 cups fine meal	½ teaspoon salt
½ cup pancake flour	Milk

Mix dry ingredients with milk to spooning (not runny) consistency. Cover bottom of frying pan with grease and heat to sizzling. Spoon into pan two tablespoons batter for each patty, cook until brown, flip, and brown other side.

NOTE: The two variables here are the consistency of the batter and the frying temperature. If the pan is too cold, the batter soaks up too much grease; if the batter is too thin, it runs all over the pan.

Baked Cornbread

3 *cups meal*	1 *teaspoon soda*
1 *teaspoon salt*	1 *tbsp. melted shortening*
2 *cups buttermilk*	2 *beaten eggs*

Mix meal and salt. Dissolve soda in buttermilk and add to meal and salt. Add shortening and eggs. Pour in greased pan and bake at 450° until done through and brown on top.

Yeast Cornbread

2 *cups meal*	1 *teaspoon salt*
½ *yeast cake*	2 *cups warm water*

Dissolve yeast in one cup warm water. Mix meal and salt and one cup warm water to make thin batter. Add yeast mixture to batter and pour in greased pan. Let rise for four hours at room temperature. Bake at 450° until done through and brown on top.

Here is a true Southern recipe, which is great with stews, chowders, and fish:

Crackling Cornbread

2 *cups meal*   ½ *teaspoon salt*
1 *teaspoon soda*   1 *cup buttermilk*
                    1 *cup cracklings*

Mix dry ingredients and add buttermilk. Break cracklings into small chunks and mix into batter. Bake at 450° about twenty-five minutes, or until done through and brown on top.

Add Liberal Quantities of
Fresh Air and Sunshine

OUT IN THE BLUE WATER ON A FALL DAY, THE KING MACKEREL GET
so hungry they try to pull you in, instead of vice versa. On such
a day, the fisherman gets as hungry as the fish; and a can of
sardines becomes a feast when seasoned by salt air, a fresh

breeze, and the kind, fall sun. I trapped blackfish through one autumn season. While it's not a bad way to make a dollar, it is hard work when the boat is not equipped with a power winch.

A blackfish boat carries a dozen or more wire basket traps which fish can enter but from which they cannot escape. Each trap is lowered to a rocky bottom and marked with a buoy. When all the traps have been set, the fisherman begins hauling traps, by hand if there is no power aboard, from about seventy feet of clear, green water. You can see the trap coming a long way down; and if it is mostly black, you know you have a good catch. Sometimes there'll be fifty pounds or more of fish in one trap.

To lure the blackfish into the trap, a few pounds of frozen menhaden is stuffed into the bait pocket. When the trap is hauled on deck, the feeding blackfish gasp and spit out half-chewed particles of menhaden. Pulverized bait and natural slime from the fish soon coat all deck surfaces and make them treacherously slick; and the smell of fish is fresh, but potent.

Still, after a morning's work beginning at about four, with the boat drifting in the seas, power off, food combines with liberal quantities of sea air and sunshine to become something that can never be duplicated at a banquet table.

Not everyone can, or would want to, have lunch on a blackfish boat with a few hundred pounds of fish stacked in boxes on the deck; but outdoor cooking—the back-yard barbecue—is so common as to have become trite, at least in the cartoons. In reality, eating outdoors is a continuing pleasure available to most and never more enjoyable than when spending time at the shore. A few grains of sand from a sunlit or moonlit beach seem to add flavor to food. The deck of a drifting or anchored boat makes a fine dining room. The back yard or the screened-in porch of a beach cottage will serve nicely for a cookout.

Here in Brunswick County, you can tell it's fall by the smell of cooking mullet. Charcoaled mullet makes one of the worst-smelling outdoor meals because the fish is cooked with scales and skin on, the skin turned down toward the coals. The taste, unlike the smell, is delicious. I was introduced to this underrated delicacy by Dan'l Walker, onetime manager of the town of Long Beach. Dan'l was a promotion-minded town manager, who worked fantastically long hours and was always looking for a way to get a coastal news story in an upstate newspaper. He was a wildly enthusiastic photographer, who burned up tons of film. Unfortunately, there was something atilt in Dan'l's eyeglasses, for most of his pictures seemed to be slanted, running downhill. But there are those—I among them—who think that Dan'l and his publicity helped Long Beach grow into what it is today—a booming, friendly, sometimes crowded family resort area which is, perhaps, spreading a bit too far these days, with too little thought of the future.

One of Dan'l's ideas was to make the mullet, an unglamorous fish, more desirable for table use all over the state. Dan'l used to say (still does, probably, because he's not past tense, although I've used it in speaking of him because Long Beach no longer enjoys his services) that if every family in Piedmont North Carolina would have just one mullet cookout a year, the economy of the coast would be given a valuable shot in the fish net.

In the early fall, when the fat September mullet start south, you can stand on the strand and watch them swimming in the wave crests, out there just beyond the first line of breakers. It's a river of fish, miles long and hundreds of yards wide at times, and it's fairly easy to tap. All you have to do is pull a haul net in front of that river of fish, and the big, fat mullet rush into the net by the hundreds. It is so easy to fill a net with mullet during the fall migration that a fisherman has to move fast to make a dollar. In early September the price of mullet to the fisherman may be, say, ten cents. So the first few fishermen who get a net into the September mullet do well; but the next day the market price may have fallen to four cents, and the day after that there will be no takers for mullet. The market becomes glutted quickly when net fishermen start hauling in hundreds of jumping pounds of fish at a time.

Mullet come too much at once. The problem is not peculiar to North Carolina, either. A few years back, the promotion-minded state of Florida tried to encourage the eating of mullet by changing the name of the fish. Mullet sounds so unappetizing. Now some people call a mullet a Lisa in Florida; and I don't know, for sure, whether people eat more Lisas than they used to eat mullets.

Well, old Dan'l Walker was trying to do something about that surplus of plenty, too. He fed charcoaled mullet to the Volunteer Fire Department, and he fed charcoaled mullet to church groups and visiting hunters and fishermen and local and county dignitaries and anyone else whom he could corner long enough to get him near a charcoal grill in the early fall. One of Dan'l's charcoaled mullet dinners was worth a million words, because the mullet still does not have a sterling reputation like that of a speckled trout or a kingfish; but a mullet, cooked properly while fresh, is as good as any fish there is.

Charcoaled Mullet à la Dan'l Walker

Fresh mullet	*Charcoal fire*
Butter	*Salt*

To clean mullet, cut off head. Eviscerate by taking out entire stomach pouch. Wash. Slice fish lengthwise down the backbone.

Fold out and lay fish flat on charcoal grill, scales down. Cook over low fire without turning, basting with small amount of butter. Cook until flesh flakes easily under tines of fork. Salt to taste.

Simple? Sure. And one of the finest seafood treats. The smell, at first, is that of burning fish; but the scales and skin form a cooking container in which the soft, sweet flesh cooks to a tender goodness.

Although charcoaled mullet is best in the fall, when the south-ward migration makes mullet plentiful, I have tossed a net in the chill weather of early spring for the small mullet of the creeks. I must confess that at this point my research is not com-plete. I know that there are September mullet and popping mul-let, that the fall mullets are large, and that the popping mullets of the creeks are small. I promise to find out if they're one and the same. I do know that the little poppers can be charcoaled successfully in the spring and summer when the fat September mullet are not available.

Mullet can be frozen, of course; but, to me, freezing seems to be less successful with mullet than with some other fish. Short-term freezing, say a week or two, is fine and seems to affect the taste very little. But a mullet that has been frozen very long de-velops a strong, fishy taste.

To deep-fry seafood outdoors, I use a special rig that has an enclosed firebox of cast iron under a heavy iron grill, which sup-ports an ovate cast-iron pot deep enough to hold cooking oil for frying. I've seen this type of outdoor deep-fat fryer on sale at various places; so if cooking outside is a regular thing for you, this type of pot is available and is a good investment. The cook-ing pot fits directly over the fire, thus concentrating the heat where it should be, under the oil. The firebox has grates which can be opened and closed to help regulate the fire and the heat.

The most common goof in frying seafood outdoors is a lack of sufficient heat. The 375° cooking temperature for deep-fat frying is as necessary outdoors as in, and it is not at all easy to make and hold a fire that hot in a charcoal grill. The oil must be kept hot enough to sizzle a piece of potato vigorously.

LET'S TALK ABOUT GRILLS AND CHARCOAL FIRES

I like charcoal cooking. With everything from hamburger to steak to fish, cooking over open heat tends to force out the surplus oils and fats, leaving the natural flavor of the food. I also extend my preference for simplicity in seasoning to charcoal cooking, using butter to baste fish and sometimes adding a taste of Tabasco or Worcestershire while cooking and just a sprinkle of salt.

In broiling outdoors, almost any charcoal grill may be used. The fish may be placed directly on the grill over the fire, as with charcoaled mullet, or they may be wrapped in foil first. For cooking steaks of fish, a grill equipped with hinged wire holders is helpful. The holder supports the fish on two sides and makes turning easy.

Lining the bottom of the grill with heavy aluminum foil will reflect heat and help keep the bottom of the grill from corroding. A layer of gravel over the foil will make for even heat distribution and will allow the fire to breathe.

When a pile of charcoal briquets is fired with starter fluid, it takes about two beers, or forty-five minutes, before the fire is ready to cook. Most people start cooking too soon; and when the fire has burned down to its best, even cooking stage, the cooking is already finished. Before the charcoal is spread, it should be well covered with ash. The firebed should extend slightly beyond the edge of what's cooking.

Some outdoor chefs complicate the charcoaling operation with hickory or other wood chips. I've heard alarmists say that smoking with wood chips contributes to the possibility of cancer. I don't try to add smoke to the charcoaling operation, but not for that reason. It can be done, however, by soaking wood chips in water for about a half hour before using them, so that they do not burn fast but make a great deal of smoke.

The heat of the fire will vary from time to time, so it's hard to give exact cooking times. It's easy to overcook food when cooking outdoors, especially at night in a dim light. When broiling a fish, cook him until he flakes easily. Generally, an unwrapped fish will cook in about five to ten minutes.

Perhaps one of the simplest outdoor meals is Steamed Clams, Yams, and Roastin' Ears. See recipe on page 14. Equipment for this feast is limited to a lard can, whereas having a charcoal cookout may require carrying the grill, the charcoal, the starter fluid, and the eating utensils.

Surfside Spot

Freshly caught spots	*Onion, chopped*
Salt	*Parsley, minced*
Black pepper to taste	*Bacon strips, cut in half*

Dress spots, clean, and dry on paper towels. Cut piece of aluminum foil for each fish. Grease foil lightly. (May be greased by rubbing bacon strips on foil.) Place fish in center of foil and sprinkle on salt, pepper, onions, and parsley. Top with strip of bacon. Fold foil around fish tightly and cook for ten to fifteen minutes, or until fish flakes when tested.

NOTE: This is an all-purpose recipe which works well with other small fish such as pigfish, croaker, drum, or bluefish. For more natural flavor, leave out onion and parsley.

Kingfish in Foil

About two lbs. kingfish fillets	2 tablespoons lemon juice
2 green peppers, sliced	2 tablespoons salt
2 onions, sliced	1 teaspoon paprika
¼ cup melted butter	Black pepper to taste

Cut fillets into serving pieces. Cut pieces of aluminum foil, about a foot square, and grease lightly. Place fillets, skin down, on foil. Top with green pepper and onions. Make a sauce of remaining ingredients and pour over fish. Wrap fish tightly in foil and grill about five inches from well-seasoned firebed for forty-five to sixty minutes, or until fish flakes easily.

NOTE: This is another all-purpose recipe which will work well with any large fish cut into fillets. Again, for a more natural taste, leave out the pepper and onion. This type of foil cooking will also serve nicely indoors for baking wrapped fillets in the oven.

Charcoal-Grilled Red Snapper Steaks

About 2 pounds red snapper steaks	2 teaspoons salt
½ cup cooking oil	½ teaspoon Worcestershire
¼ cup lemon juice	¼ tsp. pepper (or to taste)
	Dash Tabasco
Paprika	

Cut steaks into serving pieces and place in greased hinged wire grills. Make a sauce of remaining ingredients, except the paprika. Cook fish about four inches from well-seasoned firebed, basting with the sauce, about eight minutes. Turn and cook about ten minutes longer, basting with the sauce. Sprinkle on paprika. Fish is ready when it flakes under tines of fork.

NOTE: King, Spanish mackerel, Atlantic mackerel, swordfish, sailfish, and shark can all be steaked and grilled. In fact, the steaks and fillets of any large fish can be charcoal grilled. The special hinged wire grills make the job easier; but steaks may be cooked directly over a horizontal grill if care is used in turning. Seasoning ingredients may be limited to a bit of butter or oil for basting and a touch of salt.

Charcoal-Broiled Scallops

2 pounds scallops	2 teaspoons salt
½ cup melted fat or oil	Pepper to taste
¼ cup lemon juice	½ pound sliced bacon
	Paprika

Place scallops in bowl. Make a sauce of oil, lemon juice, salt, and pepper. Pour over scallops and let stand for thirty minutes, mixing occasionally. Cut bacon in half lengthwise and then crosswise. Wrap scallops in bacon and secure with toothpicks. Placed in oiled, hinged grill and sprinkle with paprika. Cook four inches from coals about five minutes, basting with the remaining sauce. Turn and cook about five more minutes, or until bacon is crisp.

Scallop Kabobs

1 *pound scallops*	¼ *cup cooking oil*
1 *can pineapple chunks*	¼ *cup lemon juice*
1 *4-ounce can button mush-*	¼ *cup parsley, minced*
rooms, drained	¼ *cup soy sauce*
1 *green pepper, cut into*	½ *teaspoon salt*
1-inch squares	*Pepper to taste*

12 *slices bacon*

Put scallops, pineapple, mushrooms, and green pepper in bowl.
Make a sauce of oil, lemon juice, parsley, soy sauce, salt, and
pepper and pour over mixture in bowl. Let stand for thirty minutes, mixing occasionally. Fry bacon until cooked but not crisp,
and cut each slice in half. Skewer scallops, pineapple, mushrooms, green pepper, and bacon. Repeat sequence until skewers
are full. Cook about four inches from coals for five minutes, turn
and cook for five more minutes, basting with the sauce, until
bacon is crisp.

Shrimp Kabobs

Substitute shrimp, preferably large ones, for scallops in the
preceding recipe.

Fillets with Tomato Sauce and Sherry

2 *pounds fillets (king, blue,*	1 *8-ounce can tomato sauce*
trout, etc.)	2 *tablespoons sherry*
2 *tablespoons onions, chopped*	½ *teaspoon salt*
1 *clove garlic, minced*	¼ *teaspoon oregano*
2 *tablespoons cooking oil*	*Dash Tabasco*

Black pepper to taste

Cook onions and garlic in oil until tender. Add remaining ingredients, except fish, and simmer for five minutes, stirring occasionally. Place fillets in baking dish and pour the sauce over them. Let stand for thirty minutes, turning once. Cook fillets in oiled, hinged wire grill about four inches from bed of coals for eight minutes, basting with the sauce. Turn and cook for seven to ten minutes, basting, until fish flakes easily.

Butter-Broiled Shrimp

1 *pound shrimp, peeled*   1 *stick butter*
Garlic salt

Melt butter and add a dash or two of garlic salt. Dip shrimp in butter, put in hinged wire grill, and cook four inches from seasoned firebed about five minutes before turning. Turn and cook for five more minutes.

We have now reached the time when it is necessary to depart from simplicity. I should mention a couple of products on the market that are standard items on the shelves of many amateur chefs of my acquaintance, since this book, aside from being a collection of recipes and a forum for some of my hardheaded ideas about seafood, is something of a record of how seafood is prepared along the section of the coast with which I am most familiar. There's a prepared barbecue sauce called Carolina Treat and a product—I don't know the brand name—called Liquid Smoke that seem to please the palates of a great many people. The barbecue sauce is often used in charcoaling steaks from large fish such as king mackerel. Liquid Smoke is used, by its advocates, on any pretext. It gives me heartburn. However, I will be tolerant. After all, I have a friend, head of his department in a North Carolina college, who has a rating system for hot dogs. This learned doctor samples hot dogs wherever he travels, and he seems to take as much delight in finding a good hot dog as he does in the delicate, extremely fine meals his gourmet-chef wife prepares for him at home. The point is, it takes all kinds. So, for *that* sort, here's:

Fish Steaks with Liquid Smoke and Other Things

2 lbs. fish steaks (king, Spanish, dolphin, shark, bass, etc.)	1 teaspoon salt
2 tbsp. Liquid Smoke	1 teaspoon Worcestershire
½ cup catsup	½ tsp. powdered mustard
¼ cup melted fat or oil	½ teaspoon onion, grated
3 tablespoons lemon juice	¼ teaspoon paprika
2 tablespoons vinegar	1 clove garlic, minced
	Dash Tabasco

Place steaks in single layer in shallow baking dish. Make a sauce of remaining ingredients and pour over fish. Let stand for thirty minutes, turning once. Cook fish in hinged wire grill four inches from seasoned firebed, basting with the sauce. After about eight minutes, turn and cook about ten minutes longer, or until fish flakes easily under tines of fork.

Fish Steaks with Vermouth

2 lbs. fish steaks (any fish)	1 clove garlic, minced
1 cup dry vermouth	¼ teaspoon marjoram
¾ cup melted fat or oil	¼ teaspoon pepper
⅓ cup lemon juice	¼ teaspoon thyme
2 tbsp. chives, chopped	⅛ teaspoon sage
2 teaspoons salt	Dash Tabasco

Place steaks in dish. Make a sauce of other ingredients and pour over steaks. Marinate for four hours, turning occasionally. Cook in hinged wire grill about four inches from bed of coals for eight minutes to a side, basting with the sauce, until fish flakes easily.

Fish Kabobs

2 lbs. fillets (any firm-fleshed fish)
⅓ cup French dressing
3 large, firm tomatoes

1 can whole potatoes
1½ teaspoons salt
Pepper to taste
⅓ cup melted fat or oil

Skin fillets, cut into one-inch strips, and put in dish. Pour French dressing over fish and let stand for twenty to thirty minutes. Cut tomatoes into sixths. Roll fillets and skewer alternately with tomatoes and potatoes. To support fish, place skewers with kabobs in hinged wire grill. Cook for four to six minutes without turning, basting with the fat, which has been seasoned with salt and pepper. Turn and cook, basting with the fat, for five minutes longer, or until fish flakes easily.

Fish Steaks with Cognac

2 pounds fish steaks
½ cup melted fat or oil
¼ cup sesame seeds
⅓ cup cognac

⅓ cup lemon juice
3 tablespoons soy sauce
1 teaspoon salt
1 large garlic clove, crushed

Put steaks into dish. Make a sauce of other ingredients and pour over fish. Cook in hinged wire grill about four inches from coals for about eight minutes. Turn and baste with the sauce. Cook about eight minutes longer, or until fish flakes easily.

Blackfish and Tater Cake

1 *pound blackfish fillets*	1 *tablespoon parsley*
3 *beaten eggs*	2 *teaspoons salt*
2 *tablespoons flour*	*Dash nutmeg*
2 *tablespoons onions, grated*	*Dash pepper*

2 *cups raw potato, finely grated*

Skin fillets and chop into fine pieces. Combine fish with other ingredients. Heat well-greased griddle on charcoal fire. Drop about one-third cup of fish mixture onto griddle and flatten slightly with spatula. Fry for three to five minutes, depending on heat of griddle, until brown. Turn and brown other side.

NOTE: This recipe is excellent for both indoor and outdoor cooking. Any fish can be used in place of blackfish. Ground skate wing fillets can also be used.

Swordfish Steaks on the Grill

2 *pounds swordfish steaks*	2 *tablespoons parsley, chopped*
¼ *cup orange juice*	1 *tablespoon lemon juice*
¼ *cup soy sauce*	1 *garlic clove, chopped*
2 *tablespoons catsup*	½ *teaspoon oregano*
2 *tbsp. melted fat or oil*	½ *teaspoon black pepper*

Put fish in dish. Make a sauce of other ingredients and pour over fish. Let stand for thirty minutes, turning once. Cook in hinged wire grill about eight minutes to a side, basting with the sauce.

GRILLED CRABS, CLAMS, AND OYSTERS

Naturally, crabs, clams, and oysters can be prepared and

appreciated outdoors on the charcoal grill. Oysters may be roasted, after washing, directly on the grill. Clams, too. Crabs can be boiled outdoors as well as in.

SMOKING FISH ON THE GRILL

Some grills are made with special hoods for smoking. Just about any fish can be smoked, and most of them come out tasting "rite good" if the job is done properly. I've eaten smoked mullet, smoked spot, and smoked mackerel with much pleasure. The following technique may be used for all of them. When smoking, cut fish to expose the maximum amount of meat to the heat and smoke, and don't be impatient.

Smoked Fish

Dressed fish   *Salad oil or butter*
About one cup salt for each six pounds of fish

Dress fish as for charcoaling, with stomach removed and head and tail cut off. Cut fish along backbone so they will lie flat in one piece. Dissolve salt in a gallon of water. Pour over fish and let stand for thirty minutes. Let charcoal burn to a low, even heat. Have ready about one pound of hickory chips which have been soaked overnight in about two quarts of water. Put about one-fourth of the chips over the fire. Place fish on greased grill, skin side down, about four inches from the coals. Cover and smoke, adding chips as needed to keep smoke going, and adding charcoal as needed to keep heat even. After one and one-half hours, baste with oil or butter. Cover and cook for fifteen minutes longer. Baste again. Cook for another fifteen minutes, or until fish is slightly brown.

Is There Intelligent
Life on Earth?

I'M SORRY I DIDN'T THINK OF THAT TITLE MYSELF. LAMONT C. COLE, of Cornell University, originally asked the question in connection with conservation on a grand scale. In this book I've concerned myself, now and then, with the conservation of marine life. Professor Cole has larger worries. He is concerned about the conservation of all life on this planet.

It seems, according to the professor from Cornell, that man's thoughtlessness may, in the not too distant future, lead to a shortage of oxygen in the atmosphere. Marine microorganisms near the ocean's surface produce about seventy per cent of the world's photosynthetic oxygen. Cole says that if our pollution of the seas should alter the ecology of these microorganisms, we could wake up one morning finding it very difficult to breathe— if we woke up at all.

Impossible to pollute an entire ocean? That's what the industrial people said about the Great Lakes.

And there's talk about using nuclear explosions to create a man-made harbor in Australia or a sea-level canal in Central America. Opponents of these plans say that such nuclear blasts would produce enough long-life, radioactive particles to over-dose the entire world.

So is it too silly to think small about keeping our own nest livable? Saltwater marshland is being filled every day, with a resultant loss of breeding grounds for many edible species of marine life. In North Carolina, the question of state or private ownership of salt marsh is still unsettled. The old question regarding the slaughter of millions of so-called trash fish by shrimpers is still unresolved.

On a purely personal level, I hate to see a small fish tossed onto the pier or the sand when he could be returned to the water just as easily. I deplore the waste of good food fish such as skates, sharks, and puffers.

I suppose I'm as far out, in a way, as was the Special Forces soldier who, when visiting the beach a few years ago, became quite angry when someone killed a snake. "You might see the day," the soldier preached, "when you'd be glad to see that snake around. He might be your only dinner."

There is no shortage of food in this country, of course. If we don't want fillet of flounder, we eat steak. I hope the time never comes that, when we want seafood, we're forced to make do with the rough fishes of the sea, for I do like a fresh trout now and then. So I'm not preaching the desirability of eating sting-rays and snakes. I do, however, think it's sensible to utilize odd foods when there is nothing better at hand; and I've done my best to dispel the idea that a shark, or a blowfish, or a skate is a second-rate source of food. In some parts of the world, they're completely acceptable parts of the menu. Properly prepared, they are as fine as any other seafood, and much cheaper.

Some dishes in this book are there as fun things or strictly for their novelty value. Although coquina chowder, for example, is very good, I don't think it'll ever sweep the country by storm, simply because the coquina is so small. It's much easier, and less time consuming, to prepare a chowder of clams.

Some items have been left out. There is no recipe for fresh, fried herring; yet a herring fry is an annual tradition in certain areas along the coast. Men go up Town Creek, net herring, fry them—multitudinous bones and all—in deep fat until they are crisp and then eat them, hide, hair, and all. I've heard the herring called "the worst fish in the world." Those who have been on herring fries describe the fish as a crisp, burned, oily mess.

Another semi-tradition is the outdoor spot fry. The spot is a good eating fish; but the way the hairy-chest crowd goes about a spot fry somehow kills my appetite, for the part of the fish that is considered a delicacy is the eyeball.

Some fish-eyeball-and-herring-eaters have had the gall to tell

me that scalloped skate wing—soft, tender, and sweetly delicious—ain't fittin'.

I think I've already stated that I feel there is merit to almost
everything that swims or crawls in the sea. The more we learn
about the sea, the more we realize that it is a treasure house
of riches. We tend, however, to take the sea's bounty for granted.
Whether we're having a snack of sea urchin gonads or a complete seafood platter, we accept the fact that the food source
is there and forget that we are rapidly developing the means to
spoil it all. The sea has always been a good provider. It will continue to be unless we succeed in fouling it completely with sewage and with industrial and atomic wastes, unless we forget that
self-preservation, conservation, and common sense are all one
and the same.

INDEX